THE **NOVA SCOTIA ARCHIVES** AND **SELECT NOVA SCOTIA** PRESENT

Nova Scotia Cookery, Then & Now

MODERN INTERPRETATIONS OF HERITAGE RECIPES

NIMBUS
PUBLISHING LTD
nimbus.ca

Nimbus Publishing Limited
3731 Mackintosh St, Halifax, NS, B3K 5A5
(902) 455-4286 nimbus.ca

Please ensure modern food safety considerations when preparing these recipes. Recipes may contain raw ingredients that should be handled correctly and cooked to proper internal temperatures.

Printed and bound in Canada
Design: Kate Westphal, Graphic Detail Inc.
NB1326

Library and Archives Canada Cataloguing in Publication

Nova Scotia cookery, then & now : modern interpretations of heritage recipes.
At head of title: The Nova Scotia Archives and Select Nova Scotia present.
Edited by Valerie Mansour. Photography by Len Wagg and Jessica Emin.
Includes bibliographical references and index.
Issued in print and electronic formats.
ISBN 978-1-77108-546-5 (softcover).—ISBN 978-1-77108-547-2 (HTML)

1. Cooking—Nova Scotia. 2. Cooking—Nova Scotia—History. 3. Cooking, Canadian—Maritime Provinces style. 4. Cooking, Canadian—Maritime Provinces style—History. 5. Food—Nova Scotia. 6. Food—Nova Scotia—History. 7. Dinners and dining—Nova Scotia. 8. Dinners and dining—Nova Scotia—History. 9. Cookbooks. I. Mansour, Valerie, 1957-, editor II. Wagg, Len, photographer III. Emin, Jessica, photographer
TX715.6.N78 2017   641.59716   C2017-904123-1   C2017-904124-X

Nimbus Publishing acknowledges the financial support for its publishing activities from the Government of Canada through the Canada Book Fund (CBF) and the Canada Council for the Arts, and from the Province of Nova Scotia. We are pleased to work in partnership with the Province of Nova Scotia to develop and promote our creative industries for the benefit of all Nova Scotians.

Table of Contents

A colourful label for Celebrated Unicorn Brand fresh preserved lobster from George A. Shand in West Pubnico. The label includes a recipe for lobster salad. (Nova Scotia Archives, MG6, Vol. 32, No. 17, p. 46)

Introduction

Take one batch of historic recipes, add a handful of local, inspired chefs, mix well, and serve up a modern version of Nova Scotia culinary history.

Nova Scotia Cookery: Then and Now has grown out of an online exhibition at the Nova Scotia Archives called *What's Cooking? Food, Drink and the Pleasures of Eating in Old-Time Nova Scotia*. This compilation features about one thousand historic recipes, beginning with those in *The Halifax Gazette* of 1765, seventeen cookbooks published from 1888 to 1950, a newspaper supplement from the 1940s, and three supplements from the 1970s. The oldest recipes provide a snapshot of life in early Nova Scotia and the available foods. Other than what might arrive by ship—such as the occasional exotic spices, pineapples, oranges, and lemons—diets depended on what could be hunted, fished, or locally grown. And with only a root cellar to keep things cold, the climate dictated what was consumed and when. Eating local and in season—something we are now encouraged to do—was the only way to survive.

To create this fascinating resource, the Archives staff—in particular archivist Philip Hartling—went through family papers, organizations' minutes, business records, and even military materials. They found recipes everywhere. The province's 1820 almanac includes "highly approved and valuable" recipes. Inside *The Militia Laws of the Province of Nova Scotia* (1828), perhaps an unlikely source for culinary wisdom, there are recipes written on loose paper and glued in. Handwritten recipes were sometimes tucked into a scrapbook of newspaper clippings, while others were taken out of recipe books or newspapers that arrived from distant places. Colourful labels on lobster cans featured lobster recipes, and industrial-volume chocolate and candy recipes were found in the Nova Scotia Museum of Industry's collection from the renowned Moirs' Limited that made candy in Halifax from the 1870s to the 1960s. And one rather perplexing discovery was a wine recipe from a juvenile temperance lodge in Pictou County!

Many of the earliest written recipes are for desserts, perhaps because of the need for more precise measurements than for dishes such as soups or stews. These historic recipes are basic, often with the method simplified or completely missing. They may have been written with the assumption that the cook would figure out the directions through trial and error. It would have been difficult to judge temperature and cooking time since food was prepared on open fires or wood stoves. They probably had little need for written recipes as they knew their way around their kitchen with everything committed to memory. Many cooks, especially before free education in the 1860s, could not write and would have kept recipes in their head until someone else wrote them down. The many recipes lacking a precise date were likely passed through families and shared back and forth.

In 1888, Nova Scotia's first known published cookbook appeared—*Church of England Institute Receipt Book*—to raise funds toward furnishing the church's institute on Barrington Street in Halifax. It's a delightful cookbook with lovely recipe titles such as *Tea Biscuits Very Good, Sewing Party Cake*, and *Cod a la Religieuse*. An older book may still be dusted off in someone's neglected attic, especially because a cookbook had been published a decade earlier in New Brunswick, and several decades earlier in what was then Lower and Upper Canada. As noted in *Culinary Landmarks: a Bibliography of Canadian Cookbooks, 1825–1949* by Elizabeth Driver, most titles published in Nova Scotia before 1950 were, like the Church of England book, community cookbooks intended to raise money for a church or community organization.

Recipes too were published in newspaper supplements, especially in the mid-twentieth century. Some were run as contests and two of the digitized inserts at the Archives include African-American and Indigenous recipes.

To create this book, I reviewed the online exhibit and, along with Archives staff, pulled out a cross-section of recipes. We worked toward the goal of showing the spirit of the exhibit and, in particular, recipes that reflect various eras in our history, geographic regions of the province, and significant populations including Mi'kmaq, African Nova Scotian, and Acadian. Some recipes were simply irresistible because of their imaginative titles, dramatic handwriting, or evocative notes in the margins. We came up with eighty-three, many of which include local ingredients from blueberries to potatoes to maple syrup.

A logging crew eats their lunch outdoors by the shore, not far from Digby, in 1950. (Alexander H. Leighton, Nova Scotia Archives, accession no. 1988-413)

Next up was Taste of Nova Scotia, the province-wide marketing initiative that promotes the province's food and beverage industry. Their almost two-hundred members—producers, processors, and restaurants—work toward presenting the province's best culinary experiences. Taste of Nova Scotia staff matched our recipes with twenty-five chefs and food industry specialists to create a modern interpretation of the old recipes, asking if they made these recipes today, what would they look like? They were encouraged to pay homage to the original recipe, but to take it a step—or more—further by using their expertise, current food trends, and available ingredients, especially those found locally. Chefs selected recipes with a personal appeal or connection. They took their assignment to heart, giving serious consideration to each recipe—what it meant in its day and how to best devise a modern version. They are knowledgeable about Nova Scotia's food history, and were eager to participate in this culinary adventure. Their impressions are captured in brief quotes accompanying their recipes on these pages. We are also providing the historic recipes.

The photos of their modern dishes were shot in some of Nova Scotia's most impressive museums: Haliburton House Museum in Windsor, Uniacke Estate Museum Park in Mount Uniacke, Ross Farm Museum in New Ross, McCulloch House Museum in Pictou, and Cossit House Museum in Sydney. The excitement was palpable as the chefs arrived at their chosen location with their masterpieces. There were no complaints about long days of the meticulous work necessary for quality photography. The photographs, with a striking contrast of old and new, are stunning.

This cookbook exists because the Nova Scotia Archives had a vision to share their unique holdings as broadly as possible. Funding was provided by Select Nova Scotia, a provincial program that raises consumer awareness about Nova Scotia food, food products and seafood, locally made goods, and locally owned and operated businesses. Buying local makes sense for the economy, the environment, consumers, and our food producers. It's all about enjoying products that travel a short distance from farm to table at their peak of nutrition and freshness. Shopping local, whether at any of our fabulous community farmers' markets or grocery stores, keeps the dollars at home and allows the consumer to know where their food comes from. This project also received support from The Canada 150 fund that was established to create opportunities for Canadians to celebrate their pride and attachment to the country on its 150th birthday. That spirit lives in these pages as we look at our culinary past and where our chefs have taken us today. The Department of Communities, Culture and Heritage and Communications Nova Scotia assisted with the project. It's been an enjoyable, enlightening, and inspiring venture for us all.

This collection tells us at least two obvious things about Nova Scotia cuisine: how much things have changed, and how much things haven't. Although so many recipes lack today's complexity, flavours, and variety, many endure. Chicken Pot Pie, Devilled Eggs, and Cauliflower with White Sauce and Cheese in the 1800s? Who knew?

The *What's Cooking?* online exhibit in the Nova Scotia Archives could still become more representative of the province's food history and diversity. The Archives welcomes additions to their collection to expand on our ethnic food heritage. *Nova Scotia Cookery: Then and Now* is not, nor does it claim to be, the complete story of Nova Scotia food history. It is only part of the tale—and a tasty one, at that.

Be sure to visit:
What's Cooking? Food, Drink and the Pleasures of Eating in Old-Time Nova Scotia
novascotia.ca/archives/cooking

Chapter 1

IN THE BEGINNING

Most recipes from the 1700s and 1800s appeared on scraps of paper, some in enviable, flowery handwriting and others in indecipherable scribble. The oldest in this chapter is a 1786 Irish Potatoe Puding. It was found in the Commissioner of Public Records, which included household accounts from the extravagant Wentworth residence of John, colony Surveyor General and later Lieutenant Governor, and wife, Frances.

Some of these recipes come from the Almon family's scrapbook, compiled by Halifax Senator William Johnstone Almon (1816–1901) and continued by his granddaughter Susanna Almon. Others are from the Uniacke and Margaret Irons' collections. Cakes showed up in a militia order book and the treasurer's book from the Pictou County Sons of Temperance Lodge. A few recipes were typed, such as the chicken soup and cucumber preserves from the Ben Church Hicks family. Lobster, pumpkin, ginger—today's popular local Nova Scotia foods and flavours got an early start.

POTATO CRÈME BRÛLÉE

Serves 6

1 cup (250 ml) mashed potatoes
2 cups (500 ml) heavy cream
1/2 cup (125 ml) sugar
1/4 tsp (1 ml) salt
6 egg yolks
1/4 tsp (1 ml) rose water
3 tbsp (45 ml) Nova Scotia ice wine
1 1/2 tbsp (22 ml) sugar, for sprinkling

For Potato Skin Chips
handful potato peels
splash canola oil, for frying
salt, to taste
1/4 cup (60 ml) white chocolate chips

"The original recipe had no baking instructions, so I approached it like a custard. I thought of a few different concepts—a cake, or parfait, or something fun. I liked the crème brûlée the best; it's an all-encompassing dessert. And I got some Nova Scotia activity happening with our nice, sweet, ice wine."

ANDREW PRINCE, ACE BURGER CO.

Peel and cook a large potato. Save some potato peels for garnish. Pass potato through ricer, then through fine drum sieve while still warm. Heat cream and mashed potato together, bring to boil while whisking to incorporate, then remove from heat.

In mixing bowl, whisk together sugar, salt, and egg yolks until well blended, add rose water and ice wine, blend in.

Add cream-and-potato mixture gradually into yolk-and-sugar mixture, stirring continually. Pour liquid into 6 crème brûlée ramekins. Place in roasting pan. Pour hot water into pan halfway up sides of ramekins. Bake at 325°F (160°C) about 35 to 40 minutes, just until crème brûlée is set but still trembling in centre. Remove from roasting pan, cool, then refrigerate.

For potato skin chips, toss skins in canola oil, sprinkle with salt. Bake in oven on sheet pan at 450°F (232°C) until skins are nice and crispy, about 12 minutes. While skins are baking, melt chocolate chips. Dip skins or drizzle with chocolate, lay on parchment to cool.

To serve, sprinkle sugar over ramekins. With kitchen torch, heat sugar until it turns amber and surface becomes smooth. Serve immediately, accompanied by potato skins.

Irish Potatoe Puding, 1786

To make an Irish Potatoe Puding
Take a Pound of Potatoes boyl them ½ of a Pound
of Buttar Pound the Potatoes and the Buttar
Together sugar to your Taste nine eggs half the
Whites Little rose water a Glass of Sweet Wine.

RICE PUDDING

Serves 4

3/4 cup (175 ml) short- or medium-
  grain white rice
2 cups (500 ml) milk, divided
1/3 cup (75 ml) white sugar
1 tsp (5 ml) cinnamon
1/4 tsp (1 ml) salt
1 egg, beaten
2/3 cup (160 ml) raisins
1 tbsp (15 ml) butter
1/2 tsp (2 ml) vanilla extract

In medium saucepan, bring 1 1/2 cups (375 ml) water to boil. Add rice, stir. Reduce heat, cover, simmer 20 minutes.

In another saucepan, combine rice with 1 1/2 cups (375 ml) milk, sugar, cinnamon, and salt. Cook over medium heat until thick and creamy, 15 to 20 minutes. Stir in remaining milk, egg, and raisins. Cook 2 minutes more, stirring constantly. Remove from heat, stir in butter and vanilla. Serve warm.

"The original recipe was intriguing. They used ingredients you don't see often, like rose water. You see recipes with wine, but in rice pudding? And mace isn't your most common seasoning. My version is standard in Cape Breton; instead of changing flavour, I changed presentation style."

WAYNE ODO, GOVERNORS PUB & EATERY

Rice Pudding, 1800s

CHICKEN POT PIE

Serves 4

1 medium onion, chopped
2 cloves garlic, chopped
2 carrots, small dice
1/2 lb (225 g) cremini mushrooms
splash oil
3 sprigs fresh thyme
2 tbsp (30 ml) butter
salt, pepper, to taste
1 cup (250 ml) sliced snap peas
1 lb (450 g) cooked chicken breast or
   thighs, cubed bite size
3 cups (750 ml) chicken stock
4 tbsp (60 ml) cornstarch
1 small potato, sliced paper thin

For Puff Pastry
4 1/2 cups (1 1/4 litre) flour
4 cups (1 litre) cold, but pliable, butter
2 1/4 tsp (11 ml) salt
2 cups (500 ml) cold water

Sauté onions, garlic, carrots, and mushrooms in oil until soft. Add thyme and half the butter, season with salt and pepper. Add peas, chicken, and chicken stock, simmer 10 minutes. In small bowl, mix cornstarch with splash of water until dissolved, add to simmering pot-pie mixture. Bring to full boil for mixture to thicken. Once at desired consistency, pour into baking pan and layer sliced potatoes on top. Place knob of butter, season with salt and pepper. Bake at 350°F (175°C) 20 minutes until potatoes are cooked.

For pastry, place 4 cups (1 litre) flour and 1/4 cup (60 ml) butter in bowl of mixer with paddle attachment. Mix until coarse. Dissolve salt in water, add to flour mixture and mix until soft dough forms (switch to dough hook, if needed). Wrap dough and chill in fridge 20 minutes. Place remaining flour and butter in mixer, cream together until same consistency as dough. To prepare pie:

1. On lightly floured surface, roll dough to rectangle 3 times as long as wide and 1/2-inch (1.3-cm) thick. Keep edges straight.
2. Spread butter mixture over two thirds of rectangle, leaving about 1/2 inch (1.3 cm) dough around edge.
3. Fold third without butter over buttered section and then fold remaining section over top to form smaller rectangle.
4. Turn dough 90 degrees and again roll out 3 times as long as wide.
5. Fold in top third, then fold remaining dough over to again form rectangle.
6. Wrap and place in fridge 20 minutes.
7. Repeat steps 4 to 6 twice.
8. Bake at 400°F (204°C) until puffed and golden brown, about 20 minutes. Place over pie, serve warm.

Chicken Pot Pie, 1800s

HALIBURTON HOUSE MUSEUM

"I found it strange they used pork in the original recipe. But it's a good recipe for using up product, and you could feed a lot of people with it, so it makes sense. Doing it the way I did it with crust off to the side gives it a modern twist instead of cooking it on the pie itself."

AIMEE MCDOUGALL, GOVERNORS PUB & EASTERY

Chicken pot pie. Cut up and par boil a pair of large fowls, seasoning them with pepper salt and nutmeg. you may add some slices of cold ham, in which case add no salt as the ham will make it salt enough. or you may put in some pieces of the lean of fresh pork. you may procure a suet paste, but for a chicken pot pie a butter pasty is preferable the butter should be fresh and of the best quality. Allow to each quart of flour a small half pound of butter, these should be enough for a great deal of paste. Line the sides of the pot two thirds up with paste put in the chickens with the liquor in which they were par boiled

LOBSTER CANNOLI

Serves 6 to 8

For Lobster Bisque
1/4 cup (60 ml) butter
2 tbsp (30 ml) canola oil
2 white onions
1 carrot
1 celery stick
2–3 garlic cloves
salt, black pepper, cayenne pepper,
  to taste
1 tbsp (15 ml) paprika
1/4 cup (60 ml) tomato paste
1/2 cup (125 ml) brandy
1/2 cup (125 ml) white wine
18 cups (4.2 litres) lobster stock
2 bay leaves
2 cups (500 ml) heavy cream
1 tbsp (15 ml) chopped thyme

For Lobster Pie Filling
1–2 lb (450–900 g) fresh, local lobster,
  cooked and meat removed
1 shallot, finely minced
1 tbsp (15 ml) tarragon, finely chopped
1 lemon, zested
1/4 cup (60 ml) reduced lobster bisque,
  or more
salt, pepper, to taste

For bisque, melt butter in oil over low heat. Chop onions, carrot, celery, garlic, and sweat in butter until translucent. Season with salt, peppers, and paprika. Add tomato paste, mixing well. Deglaze with brandy about 2 minutes. Add white wine, reduce by half. Add lobster stock and bay leaves, bring to boil. Simmer, reducing until 9 cups (2.1 litres) liquid remain. Strain through fine mesh sieve. Add cream and thyme, check for seasoning. Reduce to 6 cups (1 1/2 litres), or until slightly thickened. Season to taste.

For filling, chop lobster meat; mix with shallot, tarragon, lemon zest, salt, and pepper. Add 1/4 cup (60 ml) bisque, folding until incorporated.

For dough, pulse dry ingredients in food processor. Add fat, pulsing a few times. Add egg yolk and wine, continuing to pulse until ball begins to form. Remove, knead to form smooth dough. Wrap and rest 20 minutes.

Preheat oil to 370°F (188°C). Roll out dough as thin as possible. With large cookie cutter, cut out rings and wrap dough around cannoli molds, sealing edges with egg white. Fry shells 30 to 40 seconds or until light brown. Carefully remove from mold. Cool and fill with lobster meat. Serve with warm lobster bisque.

This is an imaginative way to enjoy fresh Nova Scotia lobster, a popular crustacean that is synonymous with the province.

For Pie Dough

1 cup (250 ml) all-purpose flour
1/4 cup (60 ml) white sugar
1tsp (5 ml) salt
1 tsp (5 ml) dried dill
1/4 tsp (1 ml) Espelette pepper
2 tbsp (30 ml) butter or lard
1 egg, separated
1/3 cup (80 ml) Marsala wine
Canola oil for frying shells

"Was that really oyster in their lobster pie recipe?! It was pretty cool and fun, but it was challenging. How do you re-envision pie without detracting from this classic recipe? Why not take that pie dough recipe and tweak it to cannoli? Essentially it's everything in the pie in a different format."

STEPHANIE OGILVIE, BROOKLYN WAREHOUSE

Jellies & Jams
Lobster Pie

Take the meat of 3 lobsters, and cut it into pretty large pieces, Having put some puff paste round the edge of a dish, put in a layer of lobster, a layer of Oysters with a good slice of butter, some bread crumbs, together with some salt and pepper, Repeat these layers till the dish be full, Take the pea of the lobster and pound it with chopped Oysters, crumbs of bread and a little butter, Form into small balls, fry them in butter, and lay them on the top of the Pie. boil the shells of the Lobster in a little water and Liquor, with some pepper and salt to make gravy Strain through a Seive, and pour it upon the Pie Then put on the Crust and send it to the Oven

Lobster Pie, 1809

HALIBURTON HOUSE MUSEUM

QUICK SWEET AND SPICY LEMON PICKLE

Yields 1 large jar

3 large lemons
2 cups (500 ml) sugar
2 tbsp (30 ml) Kosher salt
2 tsp (10 ml) spicy chili powder
   or cayenne
2 tsp (10 ml) curry powder

Wash and dry lemons thoroughly, cut into small wedges. Mix lemon, sugar, and salt together in bowl, let rest 2 hours. Put saucepan over medium heat, add lemon-sugar mixture. Bring to simmer, add spices. Add more heat, if desired. Simmer 5 minutes. Take off heat, pour into sterilized glass jar. Will keep at least 1 month in refrigerator.

"The original recipe was hard to read! What I did was put an Indian twist on it: a quick pickle. It was my first time making it. I thought it turned out really good. I am a fan of eating the whole lemon too; I will put thinly sliced lemons in my sauces."

JONATHAN JOSEPH, YE OLDE ARGYLER LODGE

Lemon Pickle, 1809

Molasses Gingerbread, 1816–1836

Molasses Gingerbread.

3 cups of Molasses.
One of boiling water.
too thirds of a cup of butter.
Table spoonful of Saleratus
two Spoonfulls of Ginger
Flour to make it as stiff
as pound cake

ROSS FARM MUSEUM, NEW ROSS

GINGERBREAD MOLASSES CAKE

Yields 14 slices

1/2 cup (125 ml) butter
1/2 cup (125 ml) white sugar
1 egg
1 cup (250 ml) molasses
2 1/2 cups (625 ml) all-purpose flour
1 1/2 tsp (7 ml) baking soda
1 tsp (5 ml) cinnamon
1 tsp (5 ml) ginger
1/2 tsp (2 ml) ground cloves
1/2 tsp (2 ml) salt
1 cup (250 ml) hot water

For Molasses Meringue
1 1/2 cups (375 ml) sugar
1/2 cup (125 ml) molasses
1/2 tsp (2 ml) ground cinnamon
1/4 tsp (1 ml) ground ginger
1/4 tsp (1 ml) ground cloves
1/4 tsp (1 ml) ground nutmeg
1/2 tsp (2 ml) cream of tartar
1/2 cup (125 ml) water
5 egg whites, at room temperature

Cream butter and sugar, add egg, and mix. Add molasses, mix until fully incorporated. Sift dry ingredients over mixture. Add hot water, mix until fully incorporated. Bake at 350°F (175°C) in buttered pan 20 to 30 minutes.

For meringue, place 1 cup (250 ml) sugar, molasses, spices, cream of tartar, and water in saucepan. Bring to boil and reduce to medium low, cooking without stirring for 4 to 5 minutes until slightly reduced.

Whisk egg whites with electric mixer on high, slowly adding remaining sugar until soft peaks form. Add hot syrup mix in slow, steady stream until thickened and glossy. Pour meringue into piping bag and pipe onto cooled cake. If desired, brown meringue with hand-held butane torch.

"The recipe is so straightforward, so why play with it? But it is up to your own interpretation as to what 'stiff as pound cake' is. It's pretty easy to replicate; it's a molasses cake, so I focused on that, spiced it up with meringue on top, garnished with poached pears and molasses."

STEPHANIE OGILVIE, BROOKLYN WAREHOUSE

APPLE CAKE

Yields 12 slices

2–3 cups (500–750 ml) fresh,
  local apples, cut in small pieces
2 cups (500 ml) molasses
1 tsp (5 ml) cinnamon
2 eggs
1/2 cup (125 ml) sugar
1 cup (250 ml) butter
1 cup (250 ml) quark cheese
2 tsp (10 ml) baking soda
2 tsp (10 ml) baking powder
4 cups (1 litre) flour
1–2 cups (250–500 ml) milk
1 tsp (5 ml) vanilla
1 pinch salt

For Lemon Glaze
2 cups (500 ml) icing sugar
1 tbsp (15 ml) lemon juice

Blend apples, molasses, and cinnamon together in pan over medium heat until apples are soft. In separate bowl, mix eggs and sugar together. Add butter and quark, mix well. Add apple mixture and all remaining ingredients being sure to add flour and milk to determine proper cake consistency.

Bake in 11-inch (28-cm) spring-form pan at 350°F (175°C) 60 minutes or until done.

For glaze, mix together icing sugar and lemon juice. Pour over cake when cool.

A delightful recipe where you can use your favourite variety of Nova Scotia apples.

"It's a very authentic recipe; just beautiful and fits our landscape as we have apple trees. I can picture the ladies in their nice clothes making the best desserts possible. The recipe makes total sense for the time. They used molasses which is heavy and very intense, so I created a lighter cake with quark—and I put some baking powder in."

INGRID DUNSWORTH, THE CAKE LADY

Apple Cake

Take two cups dried apple, stew enough to cut easily, chop about as fine as raisins, and boil them in two cups of Molasses, till thoroughly through; drain off the molasses for the cake, then add two eggs, one cup butter, one cup of sour milk, two teaspoons of soda, four cups flour spice of all kinds. Add the apple the last thing.

Apple Cake, c. 1830

Wines.

1

Currant Wine.

gather your currants in a fine dry day, when the fruit is full ripe, strip them, put them in a large pan, and bruise them with a wooden pestle till they are all bruised, let them stand in a pan or tub twenty four hours to ferment then run it through a hair seive, and dont let your hands touch the liquor, to every gallon of this liquor put two pounds and a half of white sugar, and put it into your cask, to every six gallons of it put in a quart of brandy and let it stand six weeks, if it is

Currant Wine, 1849

BLACKCURRANT WINE

Yields 5.2 gallons (20 litres)

15 lbs (6.8 kilos) blackcurrants
7 1/2 lbs (3.4 kilos) white sugar
1 package red wine yeast
1 Campden tablet
2 cups (500 ml) sugar, or to taste

"What struck me is that nothing changes. Fermentation is used for conserving things for drinks in a way that stays the same even with all the technology. These recipes work; they had the same primary resources that we use today. We have blackcurrants everywhere. We don't have that first line in modern recipes; I liked it and used it!"

ALEXANDRA BEAULIEU,
MUWIN ESTATE WINES

Choose a fine, dry day to gather blackcurrants. Put fruit in large pan, bruise them with wooden spoon. Transfer resulting pulp to fermenting vessel (23-litre or 5-gallon maximum capacity).

Dissolve sugar in 8 1/2 cups (2 litres) warm water, add to pulp mixture. Pour room-temperature water to two-thirds of fermenting vessel. Rehydrate yeast, add to vessel. Stir gently. Fermentation should start within 24 hours.

Ambient temperature impacts rate and characteristics of fermentation. Keep wine temperature at 59° to 64°F (15° to 18°C). Once or twice daily, push down and break fruit caps forming at top of fermentation. This will prevent microbiological contamination, providing richer colour, texture, and flavour.

After 7 to 10 days, once cap is nonexistent and can be mixed effortlessly, transfer juice to another fermenting vessel. Gather remaining pulp into cheese cloth, press, and incorporate collected liquid with wine. Fermentation reaches completion when pale pink sediment accumulates at bottom of carboy—1 week to 1 month.

Transfer wine off its sediment, add Campden tablet. Leave carboy between 32° to 41°F (0° to 5°C) 7 days to help clarification process. Once sediment layer forms, transfer wine off this sediment. Repeat up to 4 times, or until sedimentation is nonexistent.

It is ready for bottling! Fine tune by adding additional sugar to your taste, dissolve in water at 2:1 sugar/water ratio. Pour into sterilized carboy. If desired, fortify with 40% brandy. To reach 16% alcohol/volume, add 12 cups (3 litres).

Transfer wine into sterilized carboy, stir thoroughly. Bottle between 25 and 30 750-ml wine bottles. Cellar your precious nectar!

ONE-TWO-THREE-FOUR CAKE

Yields 12 slices

1 cup (250 ml) butter
2 cups (500 ml) sugar
4 eggs
3 cups (375 ml) flour
2 tsp (10 ml) baking powder
1 cup (250 ml) milk,
   at room temperature
1 tsp (5 ml) vanilla
pinch salt

For Crème
2 cups (500 ml) whipping cream
2 tbsp (30 ml) sugar
splash vanilla
1 package Dr. Oetker
   Chocolate Pudding Powder

strawberry jam, to taste

Cream butter and sugar well together. Beat eggs well, add to butter mixture. Add remaining ingredients. Bake in 11-inch (28-cm) spring-form pan for 60 minutes at 350°F (175°C).

Whisk crème ingredients together. When cake cools, cut in half horizontally, spread on strawberry jam, then half crème. Put back together, dress cake with remaining crème. Lovely!

"The original recipe was not complete, but it made sense, so I made my own one, two, three, four. Let's create something with that, I thought. It's funny and easy to remember! It turned out really nicely."

INGRID DUNSWORTH, THE CAKE LADY

One, Two, Three, Four Cake, 1869

PUMPKIN PIE

Yields 12 slices

For Crust
2 cups (500 ml) flour
3 tbsp (45 ml) sugar
5 oz (150 g) unsalted butter
2 –3 tbsp (30 –45 ml) cold water

For Filling
3 cups (750 ml) cooked pumpkin
1 cup (250 ml) brown sugar
3 eggs
1 cup (250 ml) whipping cream
1/2 tsp (2 ml) each cinnamon, ginger,
    lemon zest

Knit crust ingredients together by hand. Roll out, place in 11-inch (28-cm) diameter spring-form baking pan.

Mix filling ingredients together, add to crust. Bake 45 to 50 minutes at 350°F (175°C). An autumn pumpkin, grown locally, will provide wonderful flavour for this recipe!

"I changed it completely; I put whipped cream in and more spice. I changed the dough because I felt it was very plain. I made it tastier. I love pumpkin pies; they fit Nova Scotia and Thanksgiving. And they're beautiful!"

INGRID DUNSWORTH, THE CAKE LADY

Mrs. Wilson's Pumpkin Pies, 1874

CHICKEN SOUP

Serves 4

3 1/2 lb (1.6 kg) free-range chicken
3 carrots
2 leeks
3 celery stalks
salt, pepper, to taste
8 cups (2 litres) cold water
7 oz (200 g) thin egg noodles, cooked
2 tbsp (30 ml) flat parsley leaves

Debone chicken, being sure to make slices in the bone to allow marrow to release. Slice carrots, leeks, and celery, sauté vegetables and chicken until browned. Season with salt and pepper. Add water to cover all ingredients, simmer 3 hours. In separate pot, cook egg noodles until al dente (4 minutes), add to soup. Serve, garnish with freshly chopped parsley.

"It took me a minute to realize the chicken soup was for people who were sick. It's definitely an old process. I changed the technique to make it more modern and give it more flavour. But I haven't strayed too far from it. You should always cut the bones to let the gelatin ooze out."

AIMEE McDOUGALL, GOVERNORS PUB & EATERY

A Method of Preparing a Delicious Chicken Soup for Invalids.

Take all the bones of a chicken, crack them and add the dark meat; cover well with water and stew for three or four hours. Flavor the broth with some thinly cut lemon peel; salt to taste and add a little sage tied in a piece of muslin. All fat must be removed. This soup, when cold, will be a delicate jelly, and can be melted down as required. The breast of the chicken may be used for broiling if the invalid relishes it.

Chicken Soup for Invalids, 1874

CUCUMBER AND RAISIN RELISH

Yields 1 250-ml (1-cup) Mason jar

1 medium pickling cucumber
1 medium white onion
1–2 tbsp (15–30 ml) olive oil
1 tbsp (15 ml) minced ginger
1/4 cup (60 ml) raisins
1 tsp (5 ml) mustard seeds
1/2 cup (125 ml) vinegar
1/2 cup (125 ml) sugar
2 tsp (10 ml) kosher or pickling salt
1 lemon, zested and juiced

Dice cucumber and onion. Sauté onion in olive oil over medium heat until translucent, but not browned. Add ginger, raisins, and mustard seeds, stir 1 minute. Add vinegar, sugar, salt, lemon juice, and zest. Bring to boil, add cucumber. Simmer 20 to 30 minutes or until liquid is thick and syrupy. Put relish in clean jar, store in fridge 2 to 3 weeks.

Delicious Cucumber Preserves.

Gather young cucumbers, about the length of your middle finger, and lay in strong brine one week; wash and soak them a day and night in fair water, changing this four times. Wipe, and with a small knife slit them down one side; dig out the seeds, stuff with a mixture of chopped raisins and citron, sew up the slit with a fine thread; weigh them and make a syrup, allowing a pound of sugar to a pound of cucumber, and one pint of water. Heat to a boil, skim, and drop in the fruit; simmer half an hour; take out and spread upon a dish in the sun, while you boil down the syrup with a few slices of ginger root added. When thick put in the cucumbers again, simmer five minutes, and put up in glass jars, tying them up when cold.

Delicious Cucumber Preserves, 1874

An early group of Nova Scotians cooking in the woods. (Buckley Family, Nova Scotia Archives, accession no. 1985-386 no. 562)

"I never heard of sewing up cucumbers before! I understood what they were doing, and why, but with the knowledge we have of food now, we don't need those techniques. I tried to think about what they were trying to do, what the outcome was, and match that to a similar dish today, so I made a relish of it."

BEN KELLY, KITCHEN DOOR CATERING

COSSIT HOUSE MUSEUM

CHEESE BREAD

Serves 1

2 egg yolks
1 cup (250 ml) cream
1/2 tsp (2 ml) dry mustard
4 oz (113 g) aged white cheddar cheese
1 oz (28 g) butter
salt, pepper, to taste

Whisk egg yolks, cream, and mustard until slightly thickened. Grate cheese, add it and butter, continue to whisk until smooth and fully cooked. Season with salt and pepper, pour over thick toasted bread.

"How am I going to make this? The recipe made no sense to me. It turned out super good. It's kind of a grilled cheese style with cheese sauce on top."

AIMEE McDOUGALL, GOVERNORS PUB & EATERY

Cheese Toast, 1877

DEVILLED EGGS

Serves 4

4 eggs

For Sauce Gribiche
2 tbsp (30 ml) mayonnaise
1 tsp (5 ml) capers
1 tsp (5 ml) pickles, brunoise
1/2 tsp (2 ml) garlic purée
1/2 lemon, zested and juiced
1 tbsp (15 ml) each parsley, chives,
  and tarragon, chopped fine

For Cured Egg Yolk
10 egg yolks
salt, to taste

For Anchovy Powder
3 tbsp (45 ml) Tapioca Maltodextrin
3 tbsp (45 ml) anchovy oil

For Arugula Gel
6 oz (170 g) arugula
1/4 cup (60 ml) water
ice
1 tsp (5 ml) agar-agar (gelatinous
subtance from seaweed)
1/2 cup (125 ml) water

For Sourdough Crisp
1 loaf sourdough bread
1 tsp (5 ml) olive oil
salt, white pepper, to taste
arugula leaves, for garnish

Boil pot of water, drop eggs in carefully. Turn heat to simmer, cook 11 minutes. Chill in ice bath. Shell eggs, slice in half lengthwise. Remove yolks, reserve whites. Combine yolks with sauce ingredients, mix well, set aside.

For cured yolk, place raw yolks in vacuum seal bag, seal carefully. Push yolks to bottom. Sous vide at 167°F (75°C) 1 hour until yolks are set. Chill, remove from bag, cover completely in bed of salt. Leave 2 to 3 days until yolks have drawn out almost all their moisture. Place in dehydrator 48 hours until dry and firm.

For anchovy powder, place maltodextrin in food processor. While machine is on, slowly add oil until absorbed by maltodextrin. Keep in airtight container.

For gel, purée arugula in blender with first measure of water and ice. Heat agar-agar in second measure of water, boil for 3 minutes. Blend with purée. Pour mixture into shallow pan and cool, allowing agar to set into gel. Cut into cubes and reprocess in blender until smooth and fluid. Place in squeeze bottle, chill until needed.

For sourdough crisp, slice sourdough as thin as possible. Remove crust, square off each piece. Lightly oil, season with salt and pepper. Press between 2 sheet pans, bake at 300°F (150°C) 20 to 30 minutes until crisp.

To finish, fill egg whites with sauce. Place on plate, add 3 drops arugula gel beside them. With microplane, grate 2 tsp (10 ml) cured yolk over whites. Scatter anchovy powder around plate, garnish with arugula. Place sourdough crisps between eggs and serve.

"I am a devilled egg fan and it definitely did surprise me that they made it that far back. It gained popularity in the '60s and '70s, and it stayed pretty much the same throughout time. I'm sure it was a rich person's appetizer or snack, a delicacy. I wanted to take modernist approaches to it, using food science and chemicals, and themes that have come out in recent years."

MARK GRAY, BROOKLYN WAREHOUSE

FOR LUNCHEON.—A nice little dish may be made of hard boiled eggs in the following manner: Cut the eggs in half, beat up the yolk in a mortar with a little anchovy paste and butter, pepper and salt; then refill the whites of the eggs and serve with a garnish of watercress.

For Luncheon, 1881

GINGER BEER

Yields 9 cups (2 litres)

2.1 oz (59 g) sliced peeled fresh ginger
9 cups (2 litres) water
3/4 cup (175 ml) sugar
2 tbsp (30 ml) lemon juice
4 tsp (20 ml) liquid honey

"Following the recipe to the letter yielded a very pale, hazy, sweet mixture lacking in ginger flavour. This version yields sharp ginger beer, pleasantly gingery, not overly sweet and well balanced in acidity by the lemon juice. It is reminiscent of good West Indian–style ginger beers."

HENRY PEDRO. BOXING ROCK BREWING CO.

Boil ginger in 1 1/2 cups (375 ml) water 20 minutes. In the last minute, add sugar, lemon juice, and honey, stirring until dissolved. Pour into remaining (room-temperature) water, cover, let stand 48 hours. Strain into clean container. If mixture is to be bottled, capped, and stored at room temperature, bacterial fermentation may occur over a few weeks. But because sugar concentration is sufficiently high, long storage time could lead to bottle over-pressurization.

Home carbonating device can be used for carbonated version. Ginger beer should be consumed within 2 weeks. Because this recipe is simple in ingredients and method, ginger, sugar, and lemon can be adjusted for individual taste.

> GINGER BEER.—The following recipe for making a very superior ginger beer is taken from the treatise of Dr. Pereira on diet. The honey gives the beverage a peculiar softness, and from not being fermented with yeast it is less violent in its action when opened, but requires to be kept a somewhat longer time before use; White sugar, five pounds; lemon juce quarter of a pint: honey, one quarter of pound; ginger bruised, five ounces: water, four and a half gallons. Boil the ginger in three quarts of the water for half an hour; then add the sugar, lemon juice and honey, with the remainder of the water, and strain through a cloth; when cold add a quarter of the white of an egg and a small teaspoonful of essence of lemon. Let the whole stand four days and then bottle; it will keep for many months. This quantity will make 100 bottles.

Ginger Beer, 1882

Chapter 2

NOVA SCOTIA'S FIRST COOKBOOK

The 124-page *Church of England Institute Receipt Book*, edited by "Mrs. William Lawson" and "Miss Alice Jones," appeared in 1888. Although recipes had been published in other forms before this date, this is the province's first known complete cookbook. It was published to raise money for the institute's furnishing fund.

The back cover provides solid assurance of the recipes' quality:

The greater part of these receipts have been tried and proved satisfactory by the ladies from whom they were obtained. Some have been taken from the "Queen" and "Truth" newspapers and a few from Miss Munro, of the Kensington School of Cookery. The majority of them are heirlooms, handed down from mother to daughter, and written in the domestic chronicles of the housekeepers of Halifax.

This chapter highlights the church's entertaining and extensive compilation, including salt codfish, rhubarb marmalade, and a blessed rum cocktail.

Facing page: Nicholas Doucette, farmer-fisherman, and his wife, sorting potatoes in the basement of their home in Cape St. Mary in 1950. (Alexander H. Leighton, Nova Scotia Archives, accession no. 1988-413)

GRAVY SOUP

Serves 4

For Duck and Ham Hock Consommé
1/4 cup (60 ml) chopped onion
1/8 cup (30 ml) chopped carrot
1/8 cup (30 ml) chopped celery
4 egg whites
1 lb (450 g) duck, ground
6 cups (1.4 litres) duck stock (made
   from simmering duck bones)
2 smoked ham hocks
2 tsp (10 ml) tomato paste
4 sprigs thyme
1 tbsp (15 ml) flat leaf parsley, chopped
1 tsp (5 ml) black peppercorns
2 bay leaves
salt, to taste

For Parsley Oil
12 oz (340 g) flat leaf parsley
1 cup (250 ml) grapeseed oil
salt, pepper to taste
ice cubes, water

For Seared Foie Gras
1/2 lobe foie gras
salt, white pepper, to taste

For Root Vegetable Brunoise
1/2 cup (125 ml) each carrot, sweet
   potato, onion, turnip, cut brunoise-size
splash oil
salt, white pepper, to taste

For consommé, combine onions, carrots, and celery over low heat to create mirepoix. Then mix all ingredients in tall narrow pot. Stir well to distribute egg white. Place pot over high heat, stir with flat-edged wooden spoon, dragging it along bottom to prevent egg whites from sticking. As liquid heats, protein will begin to coagulate and rise to top. Continue to stir gently. As liquid reaches simmer, stop stirring to allow solid ingredients to form a mass, referred to as the raft. Lower heat to simmer. The raft will sink and stock will be clear. Continue to simmer 45 to 60 minutes. Ladle clear consommé through a strainer lined with a coffee filter. Add salt, if desired. Serve immediately, or chill in refrigerator covered with plastic wrap.

For parsley oil, blanch parsley in boiling water 5 to 10 seconds, then immediately shock in ice water. Remove, squeeze out excess moisture. In food processor, combine parsley, 3 or 4 ice cubes, and 1/4 cup (60 ml) water. Process until smooth. Slowly drizzle grapeseed oil into purée, season with salt and pepper. Strain oil through a coffee filter ensuring clear green colour. Set aside.

Slice lobe of foie gras into 4 1/2-inch (11-cm) slices, season with salt and pepper. Heat pan over high and sear on both sides quickly. Remove, drain on paper towel, serve immediately.

Heat sauté pan with small amount of neutral oil, sweat vegetables 2 to 3 minutes without colouring them. Season with salt and pepper. Drain on paper towel.

To finish, place foie gras in soup bowl. Spoon 2 tbsp (30 ml) root vegetable brunoise beside it. Pour hot consommé to cover. Scatter with a few drops parsley oil and serve.

"I took the basic ingredients, and spun them on their heads. It's not your fish and chips or lobster; it's not something you would normally think of as Nova Scotia cuisine, so it's nice to see that diversity. They are great recipes, still around to this day."

MARK GRAY, BROOKLYN WAREHOUSE

Gravy Soup, 1888

GRAVY SOUP.

Place a layer of slices of onions in a saucepan holding a gallon, over this a layer of fat bacon, and over all about two pounds of shin of beef chopped up in small pieces; one pint of common stock, or even water, being poured on the whole; set the saucepan on the fire for one hour, or until the liquor is almost evaporated—what is called reduced to a "glaze;" then add sufficient cold common stock or cold water to cover the contents of the saucepan, and two or three carrots cut in slices, one leek, a head of celery (when in season) or some celery seed, a handful of parsley, a clove of garlic, a sprig of marjoram and one of thyme, a bay leaf, four or five cloves, white pepper and salt to taste; after boiling about three hours strain off the liquor, and being absolutely freed from fat, it is ready for use.

HALIBURTON HOUSE MUSEUM

OX TAIL SOUP.

Two ox tails, quarter pound lean ham, a head and a half of celery, two carrots, two turnips, two onions, five cloves, a few pepper corns, wine glass mushroom catsup, three quarts of water; cut up the ox tails, separating them at the joints, put them into a stew pan with an ounce and a half of butter, a head of celery, and the remainder of the vegetables, cut into slices, with the ham cut very thin, the spices and a small bunch of savoury herbs if you like the flavour, and a half pint cold water; stir over a quick fire for a short time, pour in three quarts water, skim well, and simmer four hours; take out the tails, strain the soup, thicken with a little flour, add half head celery and catsup, add the meat, boil a few minutes, and serve.

Mrs. J. H. Woolrich.

Ox Tail Soup, 1888

OXTAIL SOUP WITH WILD MUSHROOM

Serves 4 to 6

4 cups (1 litre) water
2 cups (500 ml) dried mushroom
2 lb (900 g) oxtails
salt, pepper, to taste
1 tbsp (15 ml) oil
2 cups (500 ml) diced onions
8 cloves garlic, sliced thinly
1 tbsp (15 ml) fresh thyme
8 oz (225 g) diced Pork Shop bacon
1 650-ml bottle (2 3/4 cups) Boxing Rock
    Sunken Ledge porter
1 cup (250 ml) sour cream
2 tsp (10 ml) kosher salt
1 tsp (5 ml) freshly ground pepper

Bring water to boil, add mushrooms, let sit 30 minutes. Heat cast-iron pot on high heat. Season oxtails with salt and pepper, brown on both sides in pot with oil, then remove. Add onions, cook until translucent, add bacon, cook until onions start to caramelize. Add garlic and thyme, cook until fragrant. Add beer and dried mushrooms along with reconstituting liquid.

Simmer on low 3 hours or until oxtails are tender. Add sour cream, salt, and pepper, stir. Remove from heat and it's ready to serve with toast point (toasted triangular slice of bread).

"I was born and raised in Miami and have a little experience eating and preparing oxtail. Boxing Rock is local; they're right down the road from us in Shelburne. I use their beer a lot in the restaurant. It adds depth of flavour and a roasted-type flavour."

JONATHAN JOSEPH, YE OLDE ARGYLER LODGE

SALTED MACKEREL

Serves 2

1 mackerel filet
1 tbsp (15 ml) bacon fat
flour, for dusting
ground pepper, to taste
1/2 lemon
chervil, parsley, or dill, for garnish

Soak mackerel filet in cold water about 6 hours. Drain, dry on paper towel. Heat fat in cast-iron pan. Lightly dust filet in flour, pan sear until golden brown on both sides. Season with pepper. Squeeze lemon on top. Move from pan to plate. Pour bacon-and-lemon mixture over, garnish with freshly chopped herbs.

Serve with Tancook sauerkraut and buttered new potatoes.

"Recipes were kind of bland, but that's Nova Scotia. If you talk to older people, that was it—salt and pepper, and fish, lemon juice if they had some. They used what was available. Salt cod is a staple, but my concern is the sustainability of the cod fishery so that's why I switched that. But there are alternatives and any white fish could work; there's good mackerel here."

CHRIS VELDEN, FLYING APRON INN & COOKERY

Facing page: View of fish drying on flakes in Lunenburg, c. 1900. (W. L. Bishop, Nova Scotia Archives, accession no. 1983-240-104)

HOW TO COOK A SALT CODFISH.

Take a large tender fish and put it in soak the day before you want it for dinner; about 10 a.m. put it in a large tub of cold water, skin side up, and let it stand till the evening, then change the water and let it soak until about two hours before dinner, take it out wash and clean well, leaving on the fins and the tail; put it in the fish kettle on the side of the range, with cold water, and simmer for two hours. Serve in a napkin on a large dish. Make a sauce of a tablespoon flour and a good lump of butter, mixed smooth with cold milk, fill up with equal parts of milk and boiling water, and set on stove till it boils; have ready two hard boiled eggs cut in small pieces, stir them in the sauce and serve in a turreen. Carrots or parsnips are a good accompaniment to salt codfish.

M. J. K. L.

Salt Codfish, 1888

LOBSTER RISOTTO

Serves 4

For Lobster Stock
4 cups (1 litre) water
2 fresh, local lobster (1 lb each)
1 onion, chopped
1 carrot, chopped
1 rib celery, sliced
1 tomato, chopped
1 clove garlic, crushed
1 bay leaf
pinch saffron
dash white wine
2 juniper berries
salt, pepper, to taste

For Risotto
2 tbsp (30 ml) olive oil
1 tbsp (15 ml) finely chopped onion
  or shallot
2 cloves garlic, minced
1 1/2 cup (375 ml) Arborio rice
1/3 cup (75 ml) white wine
3 cups (750 ml) lobster stock, strained
3 tbsp (45 ml) butter
3 tbsp (45 ml) mascarpone cheese
1 lemon, zested
salt, pepper, to taste
1/2 cup (125 ml) butter, melted
Parmesan or Asiago cheese, shaved
2 tbsp (30 ml) chopped favourite herbs
  (chives, parsley, dill, etc.)

Bring water to boil, add lobster, continue to boil 4 minutes. Remove lobster, plunge into ice water. Remove meat and dice. Keep tails whole, cut lengthwise in half. Then refrigerate. Return shells to boiling water. Add remaining stock ingredients. Simmer 20 minutes, then strain. Reserve broth on medium heat.

For risotto, bring large skillet to medium heat, add olive oil, onion, and garlic. Cook 1 minute until softened. Add rice, stirring occasionally for 2 minutes, then add wine. Cook 1 minute, keeping rice moving, stirring frequently. Add half the lobster stock, stir occasionally for 3 to 5 minutes until rice has absorbed most liquid. Add remaining stock in increments, stir constantly allowing rice to absorb liquid, becoming slightly translucent and al dente, about 20 minutes.

Melt 3 tbsp (45 ml) butter in small pot, heat lobster tails about 2 minutes. Add diced lobster, butter, mascarpone cheese, lemon zest, salt, and pepper to rice. Combine well. Serve garnished with heated lobster tails, cheese, and herbs.

"It is quite interesting to see lobster risotto in Nova Scotia in 1888. It's very advanced. No Aborio rice; it works with regular rice, but it doesn't give you the creamiest texture. It would come from Italy, so maybe someone travelled and brought the recipe back."

CHRIS VELDEN, FLYING APRON INN & COOKERY

Lobster Risotto, 1888

LOBSTER RISOTTO.

Take one medium sized onion, chop it very finely, and fry it in butter, with just a pinch of saffron; add one pound and a half of the best rice, and stir carefully over the fire for several minutes; then add the pulp of one large tomato, about an ounce of powdered parmesan cheese, and a teaspoonful of mushroom ketchup; in another saucepan put the contents of a tin of lobsters, or, better still, the whole of a fresh lobster freed from the shell, and heat slowly in one pint of stock; when it is done, add it to the rice, and stir for a minute together; then take it off the fire and set it on a hot plate, adding a little more butter; let it stand for two minutes, then pile lightly on a warmed dish and serve.

3   Simson's Liniment cures Lame Back.

CROQUETTES OF CHICKEN

Serves 4

For Chicken and Stock
1 onion, diced
2 carrots, large dice
2 ribs celery, large dice
2 large fresh bay leaves
2 bone-in, skin-on chicken breasts
salt, pepper, to taste

For Croquettes
2 tbsp (30 ml) butter
2 tbsp (30 ml) canola oil
1 onion, small dice
2 garlic cloves, small mince
salt, pepper, to taste
1/2 tsp (2 ml) ground thyme
pinch cayenne pepper
6 tbsp (90 ml) flour
4 cups (1 litre) chicken stock
1 cup (250 ml) 35% cream
4 egg yolks
3/4 cup (175 ml) bread crumbs
3/4 cup (175 ml) panko
2 tbsp (30 ml) dried parsley flakes
1/3 cup (75 ml) grated Parmigiano-
   Reggiano
1 egg
1/4 cup (60 ml) water
4 cups (1 litre) canola oil, for deep-frying

Place onion, carrots, celery, and bay leaves in pot. Add chicken, cover with water, bring to boil. Season with salt and pepper, reduce heat to simmer, poach at gentle boil 1 hour. Remove chicken. Strain stock, simmer 30 minutes more, strain again. Reserve stock.

Remove chicken from bones, chop finely, store in fridge in stainless steel bowl.

For croquettes, heat butter and oil in skillet over medium heat. Add onions, garlic, and seasonings. Stir 5 to 6 minutes to soften, add flour, whisk 1 minute. Whisk in chicken stock, then cream. Add some sauce to a small bowl with egg yolks to temper, then return to sauce and let thicken. Remove from heat, stir in 1/2 cup (125 ml) bread crumbs for very thick sauce. Cool to room temperature, pour over cold chicken. Combine, chill 1 hour.

Combine remaining bread crumbs with panko, parsley, and cheese in shallow dish, set aside. Beat egg with water in second shallow dish, set aside.

For gravy, melt butter in saucepot over medium heat. Whisk in flour, cook 1 to 2 minutes, add stock, let thicken. Add Worcestershire and seasonings. Place egg yolk in separate bowl, ladle some gravy into yolk to temper, return to pot, adjust seasonings, reduce heat to low.

For Gravy

3 tbsp (45 ml) butter
4 tbsp (60 ml) flour
2 1/2 cups (625 ml) chicken stock
2 tbsp (30 ml) Worcestershire sauce
1/2 tsp (2 ml) curry
1/2 tsp (2 ml) garlic powder
salt, pepper, to taste
1 extra-large egg yolk

Heat few inches oil in Dutch oven or countertop fryer to about 365° F (185° C). Heat oven to 275°F (135°C) and place wire rack in rimmed baking sheet. Dampen hands to form 12 to 15 croquettes. Turn croquettes in egg wash, then gently press breading mixture evenly over each. Fry 3 to 4 at a time until deeply golden, turning gently, 5 to 6 minutes. Keep croquettes warm in oven until ready to serve. Place on plates, drizzle with gravy.

"When I looked at it, I thought wow, that's when cooking was real fun! It's old-school cooking—boil the whole bird. The simplicity of foods back then with very little additives speaks to the quality of products. Today we complicate things; it's just that we are a little more creative with a flavour profile."

ARDON MOFFORD, GOVERNORS PUB & EATERY

CHURCH OF ENGLAND INSTITUTE RECEIPT BOOK.   51

CROQUETTES OF CHICKEN.

Half a cold chicken, two ounces lean cooked ham, one ounce butter, one ounce flour, one gill stock (veal,) one-half gill cream, juice of one-half lemon, one-quarter tea-spoonful salt, same white pepper, few grains cayenne pepper. Put the butter into a small saucepan, when melted put in the flour and gradually add the stock do not add too much at a time or let it get too thick, let it boil before adding the cream, 3 or 4 minutes will do it, add cream, seasoning lemon juice, stir in chicken and ham finely minced, off the fire, turn it out on a plate after it is minced.

PASTRY FOR CROQUETTES OF CHICKEN.

One-quarter pound flour, three ounces butter, pinch of salt, three-quarter gill of water, sift flour, lay it on board, chop in butter with flour, mix lightly with water, roll out lightly and away from you, dip paste cutter in hot water, put little of prepared meat into middle of paste, beat one egg on plate, brush each croquette with egg, and lay in bread crumbs, fry pale brown in hot fat (half lard and half dripping) three-quarters of each is enough.

Croquettes of Chicken, 1888

RHUBARB ANGELICA CONSERVE

Yields 6 1-cup (250-ml) Mason jars

1 cup (250 ml) coarsely chopped pecans
11 cups (2.75 litres) fresh rhubarb,
  chopped in 1/2-inch (1-cm) pieces
7 cups (1.4 litres) granulated sugar
2 oranges
1/2 lemon
1 cup (250 ml) water
2 cups (500 ml) raisins
8 oz (225 g) tender angelica stems,
  chopped

"I love old recipes; I found it absolutely wonderful. I read somewhere that rhubarb and angelica are a good match and we were growing angelica. We wanted to use local herbs that weren't being used. The original recipe is easy; the angelica adds a little floral note to it, but not overpowering."

BEVERLY MCCLARE, TANGLED GARDEN

Preheat oven to 350°F (175°C), spread pecans on baking sheet, toast until aromatic, about 5 minutes. Watch carefully as they are easily scorched.

In large bowl, layer rhubarb and sugar; cover lightly, let stand overnight. Slice oranges and lemon thinly, discarding seeds. Transfer citrus to large preserving kettle; pour in water, cover, cook over low heat about 20 minutes or until rind is tender and translucent. Add sugary rhubarb and raisins, stir well. Increase heat to high, bring to full rapid boil. Adjust heat so conserve bubbles briskly, cook about 20 minutes, stirring frequently. Add nuts, cook 5 minutes more or until conserve thickens and sets.

Have ready 6 scalded (dipped in boiling water) jars. Simmer new lids in small pan of hot water to soften rubberized flange. Pour jelly into jars leaving 1/2 to 3/4 inch (1.3 to 1.9 cm) headspace; wipe rims, set on lids, screw on bands tight.

Place jars in big pot with rack on bottom. Add water to cover jars 3 inches (7.5 cm). Bring to boil over high heat, boil jars 30 minutes. Turn off heat, allowing jars to rest in water 5 minutes. Remove, allow jars to cool untouched 4 to 6 hours. Vacuum seals will pop right away. If pecans are floating, just cool jars upside down. Refrigerate after opening.

RHUBARB MARMALADE.

Two pounds rhubarb, one and a half pounds loaf sugar, rhind of one lemon, chop rhubarb and lemon fine, put sugar over it and let it stand over night, strain off juice and boil about three-quarters of an hour, after which boil exactly ten minutes.

Rhubarb Marmalade, 1888

Try this delicious conserve over waffles, pancakes, and ice cream, or simply enjoy with your morning toast. A great way to appreciate our colourful rhubarb, ubiquitous in Nova Scotia!

PLUMS PRESERVED IN MULLED WINE

Yields 1-litre (4-cup) Mason jar

4–6 plums, depending on size
1 cup (250 ml) sugar
1 cup (250 ml) water
2 cups (500 ml) local red wine
1 cinnamon stick
1 star anise
4 cloves
1 lemon, zested and juiced (use
   vegetable peeler for wide pieces)

Use paring knife to poke small hole in bottom of each plum. Combine all ingredients in medium saucepan. Bring to boil, reduce heat, and simmer 10 minutes.

Remove plums, place in sealable container. Continue to simmer liquid until reduced by half. Pour over plums and seal container. Cool at room temperature. Place in fridge until ready to eat. Plums can be served on top of ice cream, mixed into yogurt, or on a cheeseboard.

"I think brandy isn't used as much anymore, so I thought we would get unique flavour from local wine. It's similar to what we use nowadays. They taste really good, but it is hard to find a plum to stand up to the preservation. And the flavour of plums blends well with orange, cloves, and cinnamon. I was planning on something on the sweet side, so this worked."

BEN KELLY, KITCHEN DOOR CATERING

94   CHURCH OF ENGLAND INSTITUTE RECEIPT BOOK,

PLUMS PRESERVED IN BRANDY.

Choose fine plums, not over ripe, prick them slightly, and place in cold water, let them simmer till nearly boiling, take out and throw them into cold water, have ready some clarified syrup, put them in and boil gently for twenty minutes, take off fire and let them remain in syrup until next day, then take them out, place in wide mouthed bottle boil up the syrup with equal quantity of brandy, pour this over the plums, and when cold cork them tightly.

Plums Preserved in Brandy, 1888

IRONWORKS RUM COCKTAIL

Yields about 6 drinks

For Infused Rum
3 pieces of whole nutmeg
4 cinnamon sticks, about 3 inches
    (7.5 cm) each
4 whole cloves
4 whole allspice
5 whole green cardamom
1 vanilla bean
1 tsp (5 ml) lemon zest
1 tsp (5 ml) orange zest
2 cups (500 ml) quality amber rum

For Simple Syrup
1 cup (250 ml) sugar
1 cup (250 ml) water

For Each Cocktail
1 small egg*
grated nutmeg and/or cinnamon, or
    dark chocolate, for sprinkling

** Please use caution when working
with raw ingredients.*

Crack nutmeg into pieces with hammer and lightly toast in dry pan or under broiler—watch carefully to avoid burning. Combine everything except rum in cheesecloth bag. Knot bag and immerse in rum. Leave one week—check periodically to ensure that it's not becoming overpowering.

For syrup, in medium saucepan combine sugar and water. Bring to boil, stirring, until sugar has dissolved. Allow to cool.

To serve one cocktail, shake 3 oz (90 ml) infused rum, 1/2 oz (20 ml) syrup, 1 egg, and some crushed pebble-sized ice, vigorously shake until frothy. Add ice to 10-oz (300-ml) glass, such as an elegant crystal-stemmed goblet. Pour cocktail over ice. Sprinkle with spice or grated chocolate.

"In this rum cocktail we infused the rum with botanicals that emulate the classic Angostura bitters. What is truly ironic is that when that recipe was written Angostura was available. And here we are replacing it with spices. The original recipe is hilarious—a wineglass full of rum. How big was that wineglass? Our modern take is that we don't tend to go for anything pre-made anymore; in a sense we're going backwards."

LYNNE MACKAY, JENNER CORMIER, IRONWORKS DISTILLERY

Cocktail, 1888

Chapter 3

AS THE CENTURY TURNS

The title page of the 1898 *Elementary Text-book of Cookery*, by Helen M. Bell, features an ominous message from a Dr. Lankester: *There are scientific principles lying at the foundation of the Art of Cookery as of every other human art; and if you neglect to apply them—if you neglect to educate your cooks in them—you must expect to suffer.*

So not to frighten you out of your apron, this chapter includes recipes from other cookbooks too: *Cape Breton hand-book and tourist's guide, Bedford Recipe Book, Tried and True: a handbook of choice cooking recipes, The Art of Cooking Made Easy,* and the *LaHave Cook Book,* as well as the Uniacke Papers and the Robert Simpson and Co. fonds. From seafood and steak, to perhaps unexpected recipes for asparagus cheese or peanut soup, cooking becomes a little more adventurous.

Facing page: Workers are shown peeling potatoes for canned chowder in the Frank E. Davis fish plant in New Edinburgh in 1951. (Alexander H. Leighton, Nova Scotia Archives, accession no. 1988-413)

STEWED OYSTERS ON THE HALF SHELL

Serves 2

12 Nova Scotia oysters
2 tbsp (30 ml) butter
2 tbsp (30 ml) flour
1/2 cup (125 ml) heavy cream
salt, pepper, to taste
pinch freshly grated nutmeg
1 tomato, seeded, fine dice
handful chives, finely chopped

Shuck oysters, save liquor and shells. Set aside.

In small pan, create roux by melting butter and whisking in flour. Cook on medium 60 seconds. Set aside. In small saucepan, combine oysters, oyster liquor, and heavy cream. Bring to gentle simmer. Cook until just firm, about 5 minutes. Season with salt, pepper, and nutmeg.

Remove oysters from cream. Whisk roux into cream. Simmer until it starts to thicken.

Place oysters back in shells, and spoon cream broth over top. Sprinkle with tomato and chives.

It's fun to serve cooked oysters, although Nova Scotia oysters are also amazing when eaten raw.

"The version of stewed oysters we did is fairly close to the original recipe. As it was, I would put it on the menu and it would still hold up. The simplest recipe can be just as good today."

JONATHAN RHYNO, LANE'S PRIVATEER INN

10.—STEWED OYSTERS.

INGREDIENTS.—1 pint oysters, 1 oz. butter, flour, ¼ pint cream cayenne and salt to taste, 1 blade pounded mace.

MODE—Scald the oysters in their own liquor; take them out, beard them, and strain; put the butter into a stewpan, dredge in sufficient flour to dry it up, add the oyster liquor and mace, and stir it over a sharp fire with a wooden spoon: when it comes to a boil, add the cream, oysters, and seasoning. Simmer for 1 or 2 minutes, but not longer, or the oysters would harden. Serve on a hot dish, and garnish with croutons or toasted sippets of bread. A small piece of lemon-peel boiled with the oyster liquor and taken out before the cream is added, will be found an improvement.

Time, altogether 15 minutes. Seasonable from September to April. Sufficient for 6 persons.

Stewed Oysters, 1890

This old photo shows Nova Scotians shelling peas or stubbing beans in Morden, c. 1910. (Nova Scotia Archives, Album 17 no. 17)

ROASTED CAULIFLOWER WITH SMOKED GOUDA SAUCE

Serves 4

For Cheese Sauce
1/2 cup (125 ml) butter
1/2 cup (125 ml) flour
4 cups (1 litre) milk
1/2 tsp (2 ml) minced fresh garlic
1 tsp (5 ml) kosher salt
1/2 tsp (2 ml) multicoloured peppercorn,
   freshly toasted and ground
1/2 cup (125 ml) heavy cream
1 cup (250 ml) shredded Fox Hill
   smoked Gouda

For Cauliflower
1 head cauliflower
splash vegetable oil
salt, pepper, to taste
2 tbsp (30 ml) thinly sliced green onion

"I was not really surprised they used cauliflower that way, but I thought I'd do something a little different—roasting instead of boiling. To accentuate the taste, I used smoked Gouda from Fox Hill to complement the roasted flavour. I love cauliflower. I had roasted the head and tried it broken up as well."

JONATHAN JOSEPH, YE OLDE ARGYLER LODGE

Preheat convection oven to 450°F (232°C). For cheese sauce, melt butter in saucepan over medium–low heat. Whisk in flour, cook 1 minute. Whisk in milk slowly and keep whisking until it comes to boil. Add garlic, salt, pepper, simmer 1 minute. Then add cream and half the shredded Gouda. Whisk another minute, turn off heat.

Toss cauliflower in vegetable oil, salt, and pepper. Roast in oven 20 minutes with fan on, or until it starts to caramelize.

Reheat sauce, if necessary. Ladle sauce over cauliflower, sprinkle with remaining cheese and green onion.

> *RECIPES.* 47
>
> No. 6. **CAULIFLOWER WITH WHITE SAUCE AND CHEESE.**
>
> INGREDIENTS.
>
> 1 cauliflower   1 tablesp. butter
> 1 cup milk   1 tablesp. flour
> 1/2 teasp. salt   1 tablesp. grated cheese
> 1/4 teasp. pepper
>
> METHOD. — Have cauliflower boiled as above, place in vegetable dish, sprinkle over it half the cheese and keep hot. Put butter and flour into a saucepan, rub down a little with a wooden spoon over a gentle heat, add milk by degrees, stirring one way all the time, boil 4 minutes, season with salt and pepper, pour over the cauliflower, and sprinkle rest of cheese on top.

Cauliflower with White Sauce and Cheese, 1898

SAVORY DILL AND GARLIC POTATOES

Serves 4

1 gallon (3 3/4 litres) sea water, or water with sea salt, to taste

2 lb (900 g) baby multicoloured local potatoes, or small reds

1/2 cup (125 ml) melted butter

2 tbsp (30 ml) minced fresh garlic

2 tbsp (30 ml) chopped fresh dill

kosher salt

black pepper, freshly toasted and ground

Bring sea water to boil. Add potatoes and cook until just fork tender. Remove from water, toss in melted butter. Add garlic, dill, salt, and pepper. Toss and serve.

"I changed it up a little. I did it like a recipe for lobster boils we do on the seashore. We boil potatoes in sea water with corn and then we add our lobster and mussels. We take potatoes out and toss them in garlic butter. I love potatoes, especially with sea water, and dill and garlic that we grow on the property."

JONATHAN JOSEPH, YE OLDE ARGYLER LODGE

No. 13. SAVORY POTATOES.

INGREDIENTS.

6 boiled potatoes
½ teacup milk, salt and pepper

1 tablesp. butter or dripping
1 tablesp. grated cheese or minced parsley

METHOD. — Cut up any potatoes left from dinner into a saucepan, sprinkle over them salt and pepper and the

PUBLIC ARCHIVES OF NOVA SCOTIA

HALIFAX, N. S.

Savory Potatoes, 1898

No. 9. FISH CAKES, BALLS, OR RISSOLES.

INGREDIENTS.

1 cup cold fish
½ teasp. salt (if fresh fish)
¼ teasp. pepper
2 tablesp. bread crumbs
2 tablesp. mashed potatoes
1 tablesp. beaten up egg
1 lb. dripping or frying fat

METHOD. — Free fish from skin and bone. Mix in basin with bread crumbs, potatoes, and seasonings, and moisten with a little egg. Put this mixture out on floured board in

Fish Cakes, 1898

UNIACKE ESTATE MUSEUM PARK

FLYING APRON PIG FISH

Serves 4

1 small peeled potato
2 haddock filets
1/2 cup (125 ml) chopped green onion
   or parsley
1/4 cup (60 ml) sour cream (or more)
salt, pepper, cayenne, lemon juice,
   to taste
1/2 cup (125 ml) bread crumbs
1 cup (250 ml) bread or rice crumbs
1 cup (250 ml) olive oil
4 slices prosciutto

For Red Onion Chutney
1 large red onion, thinly sliced
1 tbsp (15 ml) olive oil
2 tbsp (30 ml) brown sugar
1/2 tsp (2 ml) red chili flakes
1/2 tsp (2 ml) garlic powder
salt, pepper, to taste
1/2 cup (125 ml) raspberry vinegar

Preheat oven to 350°F (175°C). In small pot, cook peeled potato 15 minutes, remove from water and cool. Place haddock on baking tray lined with parchment paper. Bake about 15 minutes. Remove haddock, chop, and place in bowl.

Shred potato, mix with haddock. Add onion or parsley, sour cream, spices, lemon juice, and first amount of crumbs. Mix well, adjust seasonings. If mixture is too wet, add bread crumbs. If too dry, add sour cream. Form into patties, sprinkle with additional crumbs. Heat oil in frying pan, place fish cakes, sear until golden. Remove, wrap in prosciutto.

For chutney, heat oil in pot. Sauté onions until brown, add sugar, caramelize 2 to 3 minutes. Add seasonings and vinegar, cook 20 minutes until most liquid is gone. Taste, pour into Mason jar while hot, tighten lid. Serve on fish cakes. Place in fridge after opening. (Will store unopened on shelf for up to 6 months.)

"The old recipe is basically what I do, but I wrap a piece of prosciutto around my fish cakes. I'm a pork guy; I like the combination of pork and fish. I like haddock with a little sour cream and shred the potatoes instead of mashing them. It's a more modern version of it."

CHRIS VELDEN, FLYING APRON INN & COOKERY

STEWED STEAK WITH VEGETABLES

Serves 2

2 12-oz (340-g) brisket steaks
1 tbsp oil, for frying, if needed
salt, pepper, to taste
2 cups (500 ml) diced onions
1/2 cup (125 ml) whole garlic cloves
1 tbsp (15 ml) fresh rosemary
2 cups (500 ml) Luckett Black Cab,
 or cabernet of choice
1 cup (250 ml) beef stock or bouillon
1 cup (250 ml) carrots, julienned

Place well-seasoned cast-iron pan over high heat. Season brisket steaks with salt and pepper. Once pan starts to smoke, add steaks, brown on both sides. Remove steaks and reduce heat. Add onions, cook until caramelized, stirring every so often. Add garlic and rosemary, cook 1 minute. Add red wine and beef stock to pan, stir. Return steak to pan, simmer 3 hours or until steaks are tender. Add carrots, simmer 5 minutes more.

"It was interesting, I followed suit to the recipe but I had a little black cabernet left from a food and wine event and it turned out spectacular. We grind our own brisket for our burgers here, and it's a favourite cut of meat. I'm not a big turnip fan, so I left that out. I put garlic in. It was a simpler time."

JONATHAN JOSEPH, YE OLDE ARGYLER LODGE

No. 2. STEAK STEWED WITH VEGETABLES.

INGREDIENTS.

1 lb. steak
½ small onion
½ small turnip
1 teasp. ketchup

1 level tablesp. butter or fat
½ a medium carrot
1 teasp. cornstarch, salt, and pepper
1 cup water

Steak Stewed with Vegetables, 1898

Shepherd's Pie. 1898

No. 10. SHEPHERD'S PIE.

INGREDIENTS.

1 cup cold meat minced	1½ cups (8) potatoes boiled and
¼ small onion	mashed
½ tablesp. butter	¼ cup gravy or stock
½ teasp. salt	¼ cup milk
¼ teasp. pepper	

METHOD.— Free meat from skin or bone and mince finely. Mix with it the onion, also minced, the salt, pepper, and gravy. Have potatoes nicely boiled and smoothly mashed. If cold, heat milk and butter and mix into potatoes, keeping back 2 tablesp. to smooth over top of pie. Put a layer of potato in bottom of a deep pie dish, put in the meat, and then cover over with rest of potato. Dip a broad knife in the milk kept over, and smooth the top. Mark round edges and over the top with the knife. Set in moderate oven 10 minutes, browning nicely on top.

DECONSTRUCTED SHEPHERD'S PIE

Serves 4

For Lamb
2 lb (900 g) Nova Scotia minced lamb
1 cup (250 ml) local red wine
   (Marechal Foch)
1/2 red onion, minced
2 cloves garlic, minced
1 cinnamon stick
salt, pepper, to taste

For Cauliflower Purée
1 head cauliflower, chopped
2 cups (500 ml) whipping cream
1 tbsp (15 ml) butter
salt, pepper, to taste

For Vegetables
1 lb (450 g) heirloom carrots
1/2 lb (225 g) French beans
1 tbsp (15 ml) butter
salt, pepper, to taste
few sprigs fresh rosemary
3 cups (375 ml) lamb stock

Brown lamb, remove from pan. Return pan to heat, add onion, garlic, and cinnamon stick. Cook until onions are translucent, add red wine to deglaze pan. Cook until wine has reduced by half. Add salt and pepper, simmer until meat is tender and sauce thickens.

For purée, boil cauliflower with water to cover until tender, drain, reserve 1 cup (250 ml) liquid. Add whipping cream, butter, salt, and pepper, blend until smooth.

Chop carrots and beans in large chunks, blanch, toss with butter, salt, and pepper.

Arrange ingredients individually on plate, garnish with rosemary.

Add lamb stock.

"I thought it was very simple and comforting when I read it. I thought I'd do an interesting twist on an old recipe, especially with people now preferring cauliflower to potato. This looks more visually appealing to me, showcased all the ingredients instead of all in one dish. It's nice to use local ingredients."

TAMMY McKEARNEY, LANE'S PRIVATEER INN

HARD APPLE CIDER

Yields 5 to 5.2 gallons (18 to 20 litres)

40–50 lbs (18–22 kg) apples, any variety, or 5 gallons (18 litres) preservative-free apple juice

2 packages champagne yeast

5 1/2 tbsp (76 g) sugar (approx)

"I really stretched this and made apple cider. They didn't need a recipe for apple cider then! We've made apple cider since forever; people who first arrived here brought apple and apple seeds and we've been coming back to the wild apple trees. We're going back in time; it's very traditional."

ALEXANDRA BEAULIEU, MUWIN ESTATES WINE

Crush and press apples. Collect juice in 6-gallon (23-litre) fermenting vessel. Fill to two-thirds. Rehydrate yeast, add to vessel. Stir gently. Fermentation starts within 24 hours.

Ambient temperature impacts rate and characteristics of fermentation. Keep cider temperature 55° to 64°F (13° to 18°C). Allow cider to ferment to dryness (specific gravity ≤ 1.000), about 1 week to 3 months. Signs of completion include diminution of activity and accumulation of white sediment layer at vessel bottom.

Once fermentation is completed, transfer cider off its sediment to sanitized vessel. If possible, leave carboy between 32° to 41°F (0° to 5°C) 7 days to help clarification. Once sediment layer reforms, transfer cider again.

You are now ready to bottle! Use sanitized beer bottles. Rehydrate one-third of yeast package.

Make syrup with equivalent of 4g/litre sugar (19 litres cider takes 76 g sugar). Add syrup to vessel, transfer cider, stirring constantly.

Let bottles rest on their side in cool, dark environment. You may test one every 2 weeks to reach desired sparkling and sweetness balance. Share and enjoy!

Facing page: Workers are kept busy packing apples in Berwick in 1941. The picture shows an apple crate marked Property of Berwick Fruit Products. (E.A. Bollinger, Nova Scotia Archives, 1975-305 1941 no. 472)

No. 12. APPLE WATER.

INGREDIENTS.

1 large red apple   ½ tablesp. sugar
a few shavings lemon rind   1 cup hot water

METHOD. — Pare and cut up the apple into a jug, keeping out the core, add lemon rind, sugar, and hot water, stir well and set aside 1 hour. Strain into a glass and serve. The sugar can be left out if not allowed. Rhubarb water can be made in the same way, only do not pare the rhubarb, and a flavoring of pineapple is very nice with it.

Apple Water, 1898

ROSS FARM MUSEUM

SMOKY BAKED BEANS

Serves 6 to 8

2 lb (900 g) great northern beans

2 lb (900 g) Meadowbrook Meat Market
   double-smoked bacon, diced

2 large onions, diced

1/4 tsp (1 ml) paprika

1/4 tsp (1 ml) black pepper, ground

1/8 tsp (1/2 ml) cayenne pepper

1/8 tsp (1/2 ml) ground cumin

1 tsp (5 ml) dry mustard powder

1 tsp (5 ml) sea salt

1 tsp (5 ml) caster sugar

1/2 cup (125 ml) brown sugar

1 cup (250 ml) molasses

2 tbsp (30 ml) Acadian maple syrup

1 cup (250 ml) BBQ sauce, preferably
   molasses based

2 cups (500 ml) Laughing Whale Coffee
Roasters brewed coffee

Soak beans in cold water overnight. Drain, place in pot, cover with fresh cold water 3 inches (7.5 cm) above beans. Bring to boil, reduce heat, allow to simmer 45 to 60 minutes, or until desired tenderness.

Preheat oven to 325°F (160°C).

In separate pot, render bacon till crisp over medium heat. Drain half the fat. Add onions, cook till translucent. Add spices, salt, and caster sugar to lightly toast onions. Add brown sugar, molasses, maple syrup, and BBQ sauce.

When beans are ready, drain, place in Crock-Pot along with sauce. Stir until beans are coated. Add coffee, place covered in middle of oven. Bake 4 hours. Remove cover final hour allowing beans to thicken. At desired thickness, remove and serve.

"I don't just look at a recipe for what it is, but the context of what it's meant to be. I always want to keep combination of flavours, textures, plate design, and what emotions you want from each dish. When adapting a recipe I wanted to stick to the basics. It's just merely to one's taste on how to change it. This is traditionally baked over an open fire; the main focus is the flavour of smoke without introducing smoke itself."

T. J. PITTMAN, OLD FISH FACTORY RESTAURANT

Genuine Boston Baked Beans, 1900

GENUINE BOSTON BAKED BEANS.
One cup of dry beans, soda size of a bean, one tablespoonful of molasses or brown sugar; piece of picked pork. Pick over the beans at night (the small white beans), add the soda, and cover with cold water. In the morning pour off the water, cover with fresh and boil till tender. Then stir in the molasses or sugar, put in a bean pot, score the rind of the pork, and bury it in them; bake two or three hours. Be sure and have plenty of water while they are baking else they will be dry.   MOCK OYSTERS.
Three grated parsnips, three eggs, one teaspoonful salt, one teacupful sweet cream, butter half the size of an egg, three tablespoonfuls flour. Fry as pancakes.
A little spark may make much work.

Curried Lobsters

Pick out the meat of two red lobsters and put it in a shallow sauce-pan, in the bottom of which has been placed a thin slice of tasty ham, a little cayenne pepper and one teaspoon of salt. Mix up a cupful of white soup and half a cup of cream and pour over the meat. Put it on the fire and let it simmer for about an hour when you add a dessert-spoonful of curry and another of flour rubbed smooth in a little of the liquor taken out of the pot. In 3 minutes the curry will be ready to dish; then add a dash of lemon to this curry (Some people do not, and cream can be dispensed with if necessary.)

Put a rim of well boiled rice around the dish if you like or serve the rice separately.

Curried Lobsters, early 1900s

THREE-CURRY LOBSTER

Serves 4

3 1/2 cups (2 400-ml tins) coconut milk,
  chilled
1 tbsp (15 ml) green curry paste
1 tbsp (15 ml) red curry paste
1 tbsp (15 ml) mild yellow curry powder
2 tbsp (30 ml) brown sugar
2 tbsp (30 ml) fish sauce
1 cup (250 ml) shredded kaffir lime leaves
2 tbsp (30 ml) lemon grass paste
1 thumb-sized piece ginger, peeled
  and sliced
1 lb (450 g) cooked lobster meat
1/2 lb (225 g) snow peas or sugar
  snap peas
2 bok choy, cut into quarters
7 oz (200 g) bean sprouts
Thai basil leaves
coriander leaves
1 1/2 cups (375 ml) steamed jasmine
  or basmati rice

Open coconut milk, separate cream on top from milk. Heat cream in pot or wok until it bubbles and splits. Add curry, fry until fragrant, stirring constantly. Add remaining coconut milk, brown sugar, and fish sauce, bring to boil. Add lime leaves, lemon grass, and ginger, cook 20 minutes, stirring, until flavour intensifies.

Add lobster, cook 2 minutes. Take off heat, add peas. Season with more fish sauce or sugar, if desired. Put bok choy in serving dish and spoon curry over. Sprinkle bean sprouts, Thai basil, and coriander, serve with rice.

"The original recipe is interesting with the ham; it threw me off a little. And cooking with curry in the early 1900s. People were travelling to India then from England, and people here would have had a relationship with England. People employed on ships brought stuff over. Quite interesting!"

CHRIS VELDEN, FLYING APRON INN & COOKERY

MASON JAR LEMON PIE

Yields 6 wide-mouth (250-ml) Mason jars

For Shortbread Crumb Base
1/2 cup (125 ml) unsalted butter
1/3 cup (80 ml) caster sugar
1 1/2 cups (375 ml) all-purpose flour
1 tsp (5 ml) sea salt
1/2 cup (125 ml) ground almonds

For Lemon Curd
2/3 cup (150 ml) sugar
1 1/2 tsp (7 ml) agar-agar
10 lemons, juiced
5 eggs
1 1/3 cups (330 ml) unsalted butter,
  cold and diced

For Dehydrated Italian Meringues
3 egg whites
1/2 cup (125 ml) caster sugar
1/2 tsp (2 ml) cream of tartar
1/4 cup (60 ml) water

Preheat oven to 350°F (175°C). Cream butter and sugar. Add flour, salt, and almonds. Mix until mealy crumb forms. Place on baking sheet lined with parchment paper. Bake 25 minutes, stirring every 5. Remove when golden brown.

For lemon curd, place sugar, agar-agar, and lemon juice in pot, bring to full boil over medium heat. Remove from heat and using hand blender, mix in eggs and slowly add butter. Pass mixture through fine mesh sieve into 9-inch by 9-inch (23-cm x 23-cm) baking dish. Let set in fridge at least 6 hours.

For meringues, using an electric stand mixer, whip egg whites with 1/8 cup (30ml) sugar, and tartar, to medium peak. Boil, without stirring, remaining sugar and water in small pot over medium-high heat until sugar reaches 239°F (115°C) on candy or kitchen thermometer. Carefully pour down side of bowl of egg whites while whipping at medium-high speed. Turn to high until cooled, about 5 minutes.

Place meringue in piping bag with 1/4-inch (0.6-cm) plain round tip. Prepare 2 baking sheets with parchment paper, pipe 1-inch (2 1/2-cm) diameter kiss-shaped meringues on sheets, with 1/2 inch (1 1/4 cm) between. Place in cold oven, turn on lowest convection setting, about 135°F (57°C). Bake until dry and firm, but not brown. Remove from oven. Meringues continue to dry as they cool. Assemble by placing crumb mixture in jars, then lemon curd, and 5 to 6 meringues. Brown meringues lightly with kitchen blow torch, if desired.

"Honestly, that recipe reminded me of what my grandmother and mother in Lunenburg would make. Most challenging was the vagueness of instruction; it doesn't provide you with temperature whatsoever or where your rack should be. Set in oven and lightly brown—and Godspeed! The primary ingredient must resonate through, in this case lemon. I tried to bring a bit of texture by drying out the meringue. I wanted to alter the crumb base but keep the traditional style of the pie; I put it in the jar so you don't have to lose that first pie slice."

T. J. PITTMAN. OLD FISH FACTORY

Lemon Pie, 1902

LEMON PIE.

One cup sugar yolks of 3 eggs, stirred to cream, add table-spoonful flour, grated rind and juice of 2 lemons, 1 coffee cup milk. Bake with under crust. Make a meringue of whites of the eggs and 3 tablespoonfuls sugar, spread over the top of pie. Set in oven and brown slightly.

ASPARAGUS BREAD PUDDING

Serves 4

1/2 dry baguette, cut into 1/2-inch
   (1 1/4-cm) cubes
2 cups (500 ml) heavy cream
6 large eggs
2 tsp (10 ml) salt
1 tsp (5 ml) black pepper
1 lb (450 g) asparagus, chopped
2 cups (500 ml) Swiss cheese, grated
1 cup (250 ml) Parmesan cheese, grated
handful fresh chives, chopped
1/2 bunch fresh parsley, chopped

Layer bread in baking pan. In a large bowl, mix together cream, eggs, salt, and pepper, pour over bread. Layer half asparagus and cheese. Sprinkle half herbs. Repeat.

Bake 30 minutes at 375°F (190°C) until cooked through.

Nutritious and delicious asparagus is one of the most anticipated early spring crops in Nova Scotia.

"How simple it was—basically 3 ingredients! When I looked at them—vegetable, bread, and cheese—I thought of a quiche or savory bread pudding. We've done historic dinners here, but I don't think I've seen asparagus. This recipe is slightly more complex, basically using the same ingredients but treating them differently."

JONATHAN RHYNO, LANE'S PRIVATEER INN

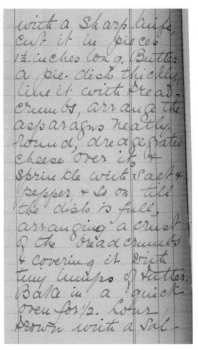

Asparagus Cheese, 1902

STEAMED RYE BROWN BREAD

Yields 5 mini-loaves

2 tbsp (30 ml) unsalted butter
for greasing jars

1 cup (250 ml) dark rye flour
1 cup (250 ml) whole wheat flour
1 cup (250 ml) white corn flour,
Maseca brand
1 tsp (5 ml) baking soda
1/2 tsp (2 ml) sea salt
1 cup (250 ml) whole milk
1 cup (250 ml) dark molasses
1/2 cup (125 ml) buttermilk

Grease 5 wide-mouthed 16-oz (500-ml) Mason jars with butter. Place wire canning rack in large stock pot.

Sift together flours, baking soda, and salt. Add milk, molasses, and buttermilk to dry ingredients, mix until just combined, with no dry flour visible. Reach thick batter-like consistency; do not over mix.

Divide batter equally between jars. Each should be filled about one third, as bread requires space to rise. Cover each with aluminum foil, secure with rubber band or butcher's twine.

Place in pot, pour cold water about halfway up sides of jars. Bring to boil, reduce heat to low-medium, cover, simmer 2 hours. Use wooden skewer to check for doneness (should come out clean), or place digital kitchen probe in loaf to see if it reaches at least 194°F (90°C). Carefully remove jars, place on cooling rack.

Once jars have cooled 10 minutes, turn loaves carefully onto cooling rack. Allow to cool 15 minutes more. Serve warm, or let cool completely, store in fridge up to 5 days.

"The original recipe is a steadfast staple, not a whole lot there that you could really change. Rye is an alternative to any of the flours in the recipe. Based on what I could gather, this was a recipe introduced by Native Americans to Europeans. I wanted to stick with that tradition. I remember growing up with this as a kid, almost a staple in my grandmother's house that she cooked in an apple juice can. You could still see the ribs from the can in the side of the loaf. I struggled with trying to find cans that were safe for cooking, so I used Mason jars."

T. J. PITTMAN, OLD FISH FACTORY RESTAURANT

Steamed Brown Bread.—One cup each of corn, wheat and graham flour, one cup molasses, one cup sweet milk, half cup sour milk, one teaspoon soda, half teaspoon salt, pour into lard pail, greased, place in kettle of cold water, cook two hours after water boils. Put in oven with cover off kettle for ten or fifteen minutes.   A. N. W.

Steamed Brown Bread, 1910

THAI PEANUT SOUP

Serves 4 to 6

1 tbsp (15 ml) extra-virgin olive oil
3 cloves garlic, minced
1 shallot, diced
1 medium red pepper, chopped
1/2 cup fresh cilantro, chopped
3 tbsp (45 ml) fish sauce
1 tbsp (15 ml) lime zest
3 tbsp (45 ml) lime juice
3 tbsp (45 ml) peanut butter
1 tbsp (15 ml) hot chili sauce
1 tsp (5 ml) ground coriander
1/2 tsp (2 ml) ground cumin
salt, pepper, to taste
3 cups (375 ml) chicken stock
1 400-ml (13 1/2-oz) can coconut milk
1 package rice noodles
1/4 cup (60 ml) roughly chopped peanuts

In large saucepan, heat oil over medium heat. Sauté garlic, shallots, and red pepper until soft, about 3 minutes. Add half the cilantro, fish sauce, lime zest and juice, peanut butter, chili sauce, coriander, cumin, salt, and pepper. Cook 3 minutes. Add chicken stock and coconut milk. Bring to boil.

Cook rice noodles according to package.

Place rice noodles in bowl, ladle sauce over top. Garnish with remaining cilantro and peanuts.

"I was most scared of this recipe, but it was everyone's favourite dish at the end of the day. That was the weird one—peanuts boiled in milk. Do I make a milkshake with it? But we went the Thai route and used coconut milk to replace plain milk. I am guessing it was originally a quick and easy dish to feed a bunch of people."

JONATHAN RHYNO, LANE'S PRIVATEER INN

Peanut Soup.—One pint milk, heat to boiling point, add a tablespoon of butter, one of flour and one-half jar peanut butter. Cook together for a few minutes, serve in cups with sippets of toast.
Mrs. C. C. B.

Peanut Soup, 1910

LUNENBURG FRUITCAKE

Yields 2 cakes

1 lb (450 g) dried Terra Beata cranberries
1/2 lb (225 g) raisins
4 oz (113 g) dried blueberries
3/4 cup (175 ml) Ironworks Distillery
  black rum
1 lemon, zested and juiced
9 eggs, separated
1 cup (250 ml) unsalted butter
2 cups (500 ml) brown sugar
1 cup (250 ml) whole milk
2 cups (500 ml) all-purpose flour
2 cups (500 ml) dark rye flour
2 tsp (10 ml) baking powder
1 tsp (5 ml) sea salt
1/4 tsp (1 ml) ground cloves
1/4 tsp (1 ml) ground nutmeg
1/4 tsp (1 ml) cinnamon
1/4 tsp (1 ml) Ironworks Distillery
  cranberry liqueur

For Cranberry Liqueur Glaze
1 cup (250 ml) caster sugar
1/2 cup (125 ml) water
1/3 cup (75 ml) cranberry liqueur
1 tsp (5 ml) vanilla bean paste

Soak cranberries, raisins, and blueberries with rum, lemon juice, and zest overnight.

Preheat oven to 300°F (150°C). Whisk egg whites to stiff peaks, place in refrigerator until needed. Using electric stand mixer, cream butter and sugar on speed 4. Once incorporated, add egg yolks gradually. Turn to speed 1 and add milk. The mixture will look separated.

In a separate bowl, sift together both flours, baking powder, salt, cloves, nutmeg, and cinnamon.

Add soaked fruit to butter-sugar mixture. Then, alternating between dry ingredients and egg whites, fold in thirds into batter and fruit base. Mix until thick. Divide batter equally between 2 greased 9-inch (23-cm) cast-iron pans, place in oven on middle rack. Bake at least 1 hour and 45 minutes. Cake is done when skewer placed in cake comes out clean.

Meanwhile, place all ingredients for glaze in pot and bring to simmer over medium heat. Let cool. Remove cakes from oven, immediately brush with cranberry liqueur. Remove from pans, place on cooling rack. Once completely cooled, brush with glaze and serve.

GAELIC FRUIT CAKE.

MRS. J. H. WYMAN.

2 cups sugar, 1 cup butter, 1 cup milk, 9 eggs, 4 cups flour sifted with 2 tsps. baking powder, 1 lb. raisins seeded and chopped, ½ lb. currants, ¼ lb. citron sliced thin. Cream sugar and butter, add milk gradually, then yolks of eggs beaten, flour, and while beating in flour add the whites beaten stiff. Flavor. Put layer of batter and layer of mixed fruit, finishing with layer of batter.

Gaelic Fruit Cake, 1912

ROSS FARM MUSEUM

"It says to flavour it. What says fruitcake? Warm spices, cloves, nutmeg, cinnamon, traditional Christmas flavours. I love cranberries and Terra Beata is in Lunenburg County. Still, at the end of the day, you need the raisins; they provide absorption, especially soaked in rum. I was a bit shocked there was no rum in the original. It produces a large amount of fruitcake. They actually state for the egg to be separated; someone was keeping in mind to alleviate the denseness of the fruitcake and provide a light and airier batter. It had more rise on it than some."

T. J. PITTMAN, OLD FISH FACTORY RESTAURANT

SCALLOP CHOWDER

Serves 4

2 tsp (10 ml) olive oil
2 slices bacon, cut into small pieces
1 small onion, diced
1 small carrot, diced
1 rib celery, diced
2 cloves garlic, minced
2 cups (500 ml) chicken broth
   or fish stock
1 cup (250 ml) potatoes, peeled and diced
pinch cayenne pepper
black pepper, to taste
1 cup (250 ml) whipping cream
1 red chili pepper, diced
1 tsp (5 ml) lemon zest
salt, to taste
1 lb (450 g) bay or other sustainable
   scallops
2 tbsp (30 ml) chopped fresh tarragon
   or dill

Heat olive oil in pot over medium heat. Add bacon, cook until fat renders and bacon is slightly browned, 3 to 5 minutes. Add onion to bacon, stir until soft and translucent, 3 to 5 minutes. Stir in carrot, celery, and garlic, cook 1 minute until fragrant.

Pour chicken broth, potato, cayenne pepper, and black pepper into bacon mixture. Reduce heat to medium low, simmer 12 to 15 minutes or until potatoes are almost tender. Stir in cream and chili pepper, simmer about 5 minutes or until potatoes are completely tender. Season with lemon zest and salt.

Stir scallops into chowder, cook over medium heat until scallops are tender and white. Remove from heat, stir in herbs. Serve.

Nova Scotia scallops are rich in flavour, unique in texture, and deservedly world famous.

"The old recipe has a base, and you know from experience it works. Salt pork was readily available and provided salt. I've added bacon, garlic, and chili pepper to give it a twist."

CHRIS VELDEN, FLYING APRON INN & COOKERY

SCALLOP CHOWDER.

Pour one cup water over one quart of scallops, pick out scallops, then strain liquid, chop one-quarter pound salt pork and try out. Add one onion and cook until brown, then pour on a cup of water and let boil five minutes. Strain this into the scallop broth and heat to the boiling point. In the meantime cook three cups sliced potatoes five minutes. Strain scallop broth over potatoes, return to fire and cook until potatoes are done. Add scallops and cook five minutes after boiling begins Add one teaspoon salt and one pint rich milk, pepper to taste.

Scallop Chowder, 1912

Chapter 4

BETWEEN WORLD WARS

Families' dependence on the land and sea was never more critical than during years of economic hardship. This era was also marked by increased transportation opportunities and immigration, so perhaps the appearance of mulligatawny soup in two collections shouldn't be surprising.

This chapter's recipes originated in the Prat-Starr fonds, and two companies' promotional books, *Kent Vinegars Recipe Book* and *Farmers' Milk Facts*. Strawberry custard and strawberry shortcake appeared in *The Modern Cookbook for Nova Scotia and Prince Edward Island*, published in about 1922. It was not the first time a recipe for these favourites showed up in a Nova Scotia cookbook and certainly not the last. Another recipe, Mable Gilson's chocolate cake, leads one to wonder who Mable Gilson was. And who was Mrs. Frampton for whom a tomato soup was named? Why was a pastry recipe called pop doodle? Historic recipes can present as many questions as answers.

STRAWBERRY YOGURT CUSTARD WITH PEPPER AND APPLE JELLY GLAZE

Serves 4

1/2 cup (125 ml) whipping cream
1/2 cup (125 ml) sugar
1/2 tsp (2 ml) vanilla
1 cup (250 ml) Greek-style plain yogurt
24 fresh, local strawberries
1/3 cup (80 ml) apple jelly, melted
cracked pepper, to taste

Whip cream to soft peak, adding sugar and vanilla after it has begun to thicken. Scoop yogurt into medium bowl. Fold in whipped cream to make yogurt custard. Crush strawberries.

Pour layer of custard into 4 sherbet glasses. Add crushed strawberries and additional custard. Top each with 2 tbsp (30 ml) apple jelly and lightly grated pepper. Refrigerate to chill.

"This updated version removes the nuts and simplifies the decoration while putting a deliciously sweet and spicy glaze on the top. I used crushed strawberries on the bottom; that's the way to go for today's cooks. You don't see the bottom of the sherbet cup, so if you're going to create a pattern, at least make it visual. The use of grated pepper with fresh strawberries was made popular in Nova Scotia in the 1980s by the late Chef Alex Clavel."

HOWARD SELIG, VALLEY FLAXFLOUR

---

144   MODERN COOK BOOK

Send for the KNOX GELATINE Recipe Book.

Strawberry Custard.

Make a custard of one and half cups of milk, three-quarters cupful of sugar, two eggs, two level tablespoons cornstarch, one-half teaspoon vanilla. Heat milk in double boiler, add cornstarch dissolved in little milk, let come to boil, add eggs and sugar beaten together, remove from stove, add vanilla. Have ready Sherbet cups as you wish to serve. Take five strawberries for each cup, cut in halves, lengthwise, in the bottom of each cup place a half walnut, arrange five pieces of berries around it, now pour in warm custard, leaving room enough to repeat the flower design on top. This may be made early in the day, as it is best served cold.

Mrs. J. N. Hutton, Halifax.

Strawberry Custard, c. 1920

Strawberry Shortcake.

Into two cups of flour put three teaspoons magic baking powder, one-quarter teaspoonful salt (sift twice). To this add three-tablespoons each of butter and lard, chop with a silver knife until thoroughly mixed; add one cup milk. Mix it all thoroughly and divide in halves, baking each half in a pie plate, do not roll out or touch with the hands, but spread the dough with a fork or knife over the pie plate. Bake twelve minutes in hot oven, spread with berries, which have been previously hulled, crushed and cured in sugar for several hours. Cover with a layer of crushed berries and top with whipped cream and whole fruit. *Ann Marie Lloyd, Halifax.*

Strawberry Shortcake, c. 1920

STRAWBERRIES IN PUFF PASTRY WITH CHANTILLY CREAM AND CHOCOLATE SAUCE

Serves 4

1 sheet frozen puff pastry
handful raw macaroni noodles
2 cups (500 ml) fresh, local strawberries
1/2 cup (125 ml) sugar
1 cup (250 ml) whipping cream
1/4 cup (60 ml) sugar
1 tsp (5 ml) vanilla
milk chocolate sauce, for drizzling

Thaw pastry sheets, cut into 8 squares, lightly perforate top layer to prevent excessive puffing.

Prepare set of large muffin cups by filling one-third with raw macaroni noodles (to prevent sagging). Press pastry into cups, leaving square edges above. Bake in preheated oven 15 minutes at 425°F (218°C), or follow package instructions.

Crush strawberries with sugar. Whip cream with second sugar amount, and vanilla.

To serve, place one baked pastry square on plate, top with crushed berries and whipped cream. Repeat with second layer of pastry and toppings. Drizzle with chocolate sauce.

The colour, the texture, the taste—there is good reason that fresh, local strawberries are one of the best-loved crops of early spring and summer in Nova Scotia!

"Shortcake is so popular; I love it. It's really stretching it to change that. The recipe was basic and good. You wouldn't make your own biscuits unless you're a home baker and want to put a personal stamp on it. So I went with frozen puff pastry; it's easy and anyone can do it."

HOWARD SELIG, VALLEY FLAXFLOUR

GLUTEN-FREE POP-CAKES

Yields 18 muffins

splash of oil for muffin tins
1/2 tsp (2 ml) butter x 18 for muffin tins
2 tbsp (30 ml) sugar
1 tsp (5 ml) cinnamon
1 cup (250 ml) sugar
1/2 cup (125 ml) butter, softened
1 egg
3/4 cup (175 ml) buckwheat flour
3/4 cup (175 ml) fine organic corn flour
1/2 cup (125 ml) gluten-free oat flour
1/2 cup (125 ml) fine flax flour
1 tbsp (15 ml) baking powder
1/2 tsp (2 ml) salt
1 cup (250 ml) milk

Preheat oven to 375°F (190°C). Generously oil 18 large muffin tins, place butter in bottom of each. Mix 2 tbsp (30 ml) sugar with cinnamon, sprinkle some into each tin. Place in oven 5 minutes to melt butter.

Cream together second amount of sugar and butter. Beat in egg. Sift together flours for gluten-free mix, or, alternatively, use 2 1/2 cups (625 ml) all-purpose flour. Add baking powder and salt. Combine these dry ingredients, alternately with milk, into butter mixture.

Pour batter into prepared muffin tins about two-thirds full to avoid a muffin top. Bake 20 to 25 minutes or until baked through. Turn out before they cool completely.

Serve warm on individual plates with Greek-style yogurt and fresh fruit of choice. Go ahead, add a drizzle of maple syrup! This is a satisfying and delicious breakfast.

"The original recipe appears to be a traditional quick-cake and a colloquial name for the more commonly named one-egg cake as found in The Fannie Farmer Cookbook *of 1896. This updated version includes the addition of flax flour, or milled flaxseed, to enhance the nutritional composition by increasing the fibre and omega-3 fatty acid content, in keeping with the current desire for more nutrient-dense foods."*

HOWARD SELIG, VALLEY FLAXFLOUR

Brown Bread.

Two cups oatmeal, one-half cup cornmeal, one tablespoon salt, one tablespoon butter, one-half cup molasses, one yeast cake. Pour three cups boiling water on oatmeal, cornmeal and salt, butter. Let stand until cool, add molasses and flour enough to make very stiff. Let stand over night in a mold in one large loaf; do not add more flour. — *Mrs. C. F. Rand.*

Pop Doodle.

One cup sugar, one-half cup butter, one egg, one cup milk, two and one-half cups sifted flour, three teaspoons baking powder, salt. Before baking, sprinkle with mixture of cinnamon and sugar. Bake in hot oven twenty minutes. Eat hot with butter. — *M. B. C., Yarmouth.*

Muffins (good)

Two cups flour, four teaspoons baking powder, one-half teaspoon salt, two tablespoons sugar, one and one-half cup milk, two tablespoons butter (melted) one egg (beaten) — *Evelyn Brown.*

Grape Nut Bread.

One cup grape nuts, one cup scalded milk (cool), one cup cold milk, two-thirds cup sugar, one egg, three teaspoonfuls baking powder, salt, three cups flour (sifted together). Let stand one and one-quarter hours then bake in medium oven about one and one-quarter to one and one-half hours. — *Anna F. Perrin.*

Brown Bread.

Two cups graham flour, two cups white flour, one-half cup sugar (brown or white) one teaspoon soda, one teaspoon salt (mix dry with flour) one cup seeded raisins, two cups sour milk or butter milk. Bake in moderate oven one and one-quarter hours. — *F. C. Murray.*

Pop Doodle, c. 1920

Salmon Croquettes, 1921

UNIACKE ESTATE
MUSEUM PARK

Salmon Croquettes.   Prize winner

1 pt chopped salmon.
2 - 3 cups cream.   Mix flour - Let
1 large tbsp butter.   cream come to -
small tbsp flour.   boiling point,
2 eggs.   stir in butter,
2 - 3 pt bread crumbs.   salmon, & seasoning,
salt & pepper to taste.   Boil 2 + firs.

Then to cool form into Croquettes, & fry
in hot lard.

COLD-SMOKED SALMON CROQUETTES

Yields 12 hors d'oeuvres

1 egg, white and yolk separated
4 1/2 oz (125 g) cold smoked salmon
1 lemon, zest and juice
2–3 tbsp (30–45 ml) whipping cream
1 cup (250 ml) mashed potato
1 green onion, thinly sliced
1 tbsp (15 ml) capers, chopped as fine
  as possible
pinch smoked paprika
pinch cayenne
salt, pepper, to taste
1/2 cup (125 ml) flour
1–2 eggs, beaten
1/2 cup (125 ml) bread crumbs,
  seasoned with salt and pepper
canola oil, for frying

"The original is a really good recipe for a classic croquette; it worked fine. It was heavier than it needed to be, so I went with a salmon mousse to lighten it up. It's an award-winning recipe so I wanted to do it justice, but elevate it a bit."

BEN KELLY, KITCHEN DOOR CATERING

In mixer with whip attachment, whip egg white to soft peaks. Remove from bowl and set aside. Put yolk in bowl, whip on high 2 minutes. Add salmon and few drops of lemon juice and whip 2 more minutes. Add whipping cream and mashed potato, whip 2 minutes.

Using spatula, gently mix in lemon zest, remaining lemon juice, green onion, capers, paprika, and cayenne. Fold in egg whites. Leave in fridge 2 hours covered with plastic wrap.

Spoon mixture evenly onto parchment covered baking sheet, place in freezer 30 minutes.

Fill 3 bowls halfway, one with flour, one with beaten eggs, and the third with bread crumbs. Roll spoonful of mixture in flour to coat. Shake off excess flour and place mixture in egg. Shake off excess egg and place in bread crumbs. Shake off excess and place on baking sheet. Repeat this process until entire mixture has been breaded. Each croquette should be of equal size.

In deep skillet, heat about 2 inches (5 cm) oil over medium heat until candy thermometer reads 350°F (175°C). Gently fry all croquettes, until evenly browned, flipping once or twice. Remove, set on paper towel. Serve with lemon or tartar sauce.

Nova Scotia's smoked salmon is second to none and is appreciated by itself, or in an easy and scrumptious recipe like this one.

LEMON THYME JELLY

Yields 6 jars

6 large oranges
4 large lemons
7 cups (1.4 litres) water
4 fresh thyme sprigs, about 4 inches
   (10 cm) long
5 cups (1.1 litres) granulated sugar
   (approx)
1/3 cup (75 ml) lemon thyme leaves

Wash oranges and lemons. Slice as thin as possible, preferably with food processor.

In large saucepan, combine slices with seeds and juice, water, and thyme. Cover, bring to simmer, cook gently until slices are softened and translucent, about 1 hour. Transfer to dampened jelly bag or colander lined with double layer dampened cheesecloth. (Dampened pillowcase also works.) Let drip at least 4 hours. Do not squeeze bag, or jelly will be cloudy.

In preserving kettle, combine juice and equal quantity of sugar. Boil vigorously until jelly reaches setting point, about 10 to 14 minutes. To test, chill 2 small plates in freezer. Drop 1/2 tsp (2 ml) hot jelly onto one plate; return to freezer 1 minute, then tilt plate. For soft set, mixture will still flow very slowly. For firm set, mixture should be firm and wrinkle when edge is pushed with finger. If mixture is syrupy, continue to boil, Repeat test every few minutes until proper set is reached.

Remove jelly from heat, skim off scum. Add thyme, stir about 3 minutes to distribute evenly. Have ready 6 scalded (dipped in boiling water), 250-ml (1-cup) jars. Simmer new lids in small pan of hot water to soften rubberized flange. Pour jelly into jars leaving 1/2 to 3/4 inch (1.3 to 1.9 cm) head space, wipe rims, set on lids, screw bands on tight.

"We were thinking of what might work with marmalade and someone said marmalade thyme. It had a ring. The original recipe would work but lemon thyme adds softness. That's the spirit of that marmalade recipe—take any recipe and throw it on its head. I grew up with those cookbooks. They show you how many influences came from immigrants and war; and people had to wait all year to get an orange. To make marmalade in 1921 was a luxury—as it was for my dad and grandmother to receive an orange."

BEVERLY McCLARE, TANGLED GARDEN

Place jars in big pot with rack on bottom, add water to cover jars by 3 inches (7.5 cm). Boil 30 minutes. Turn off heat, allow jars to rest 5 minutes before removing. Vacuum seal will pop immediately. If lemon thyme is on top, gently shake bottles to redistribute leaves. Repeat as necessary. Some may be prettier than others, but all will taste delicious!

Refrigerate after opening. A treat for breakfast or afternoon tea on soft cheese, chicken, or fish.

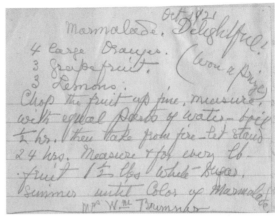

Marmalade, 1921

CREOLE BABY POTATOES

Serves 4 as side

1 lb (450 g) local, baby potatoes
1/4 green pepper, finely diced
1/4 red pepper, finely diced
1/4 medium onion, finely diced
pinch cayenne pepper
2 tbsp (30 ml) olive oil
1–2 sprigs thyme
1/2 tsp (2 ml) smoked paprika
1/4 tsp (1 ml) dried oregano
salt, pepper, to taste

Cook potatoes in boiling, salted water, cool in fridge overnight, and cut into quarters.

Combine all ingredients in bowl, toss to mix well. Put on parchment-lined baking sheet, bake at 425°F (218°C) 30 to 35 minutes, tossing once or twice so potatoes cook evenly.

Creole New Potatoes

Boil the potatoes (small ones) in salted water, peeling a ring of the skin from the center of each. When nearly cooked drain, sprinkle with salt and cover with a folded napkin for five minutes. Meanwhile fry in two tablespoonsful of hot bacon dripping, two minced slices of green pepper and a small minced onion. When delicately browned add a cupful of thickened tomato purée, half a teaspoonful of sugar, salt and celery salt to taste and a tablespoonful of chopped parsley. Cook, stirring constantly, and pour over the potatoes that have been peeled and placed in a heated vegetable dish. This preparation of potatoes is delicious as the main dish for luncheon if a few slices of broiled bacon are placed over the top.

Creole New Potatoes, 1922

"The name is odd as they didn't use Creole spices. I tried to use more traditional Creole spices. I lightened it up a bit by taking tomato paste out; I simplified it by parboiling and roasting the potatoes. The original recipe mentioned boiling the potatoes and peeling a ring from the centre from each. The only reason I could think to do it was that the salt would absorb moisture and pop the skin right off."

BEN KELLY, KITCHEN DOOR CATERING

CHICKEN AND HAM SANDWICHES

Yields 4 sandwiches

1/4 cup (60 ml) mayonnaise
1/2 cup (125 ml) leftover chicken,
 picked or chopped
1/2 cup (125 ml) leftover ham, chopped
1 tbsp (15 ml) minced sweet gherkins
1 tsp (5 ml) minced onion
1 tbsp (15 ml) minced celery
salt, pepper, to taste
1–2 tbsp (15–30 ml) softened butter
8 slices bread of your choice

Combine all ingredients except butter and bread. Mix thoroughly, season. Butter the bread, make sandwiches with filling. Cut sandwiches in 4. Serve for lunch or with tea.

"I looked at this one and I didn't even know where to begin. I was trying to stay close to the original but it is boiled ham and chicken blended with butter on bread! I essentially made a chicken and ham salad and it worked well. I was thinking of something someone would want to eat!"

BEN KELLY, KITCHEN DOOR CATERING

WINDSOR SANDWICHES

Cream one cup of butter. Add to this one half cup each finely chopped ham (boiled) and cold boiled chicken. Season with salt and pepper and spread mixture between thin slices of bread.
                                  MISS A. SMITH.
264 Agricola street.

Windsor Sandwiches, 1922

Special, Box Luncheon, Hedly Doty, photographer, c. 1946; (NSA,
Nova Scotia Information Service) photo no. 45

"There were only so many ingredients available, so they would have brought some things from Europe. This one I changed drastically. They didn't have cocoa; I made it with cocoa so it would be dark, and more baking powder so the texture would be fluffier."

INGRID DUNSWORTH, THE CAKE LADY

INGRID DUNSWORTH'S CHOCOLATE CAKE

Yields 10 slices

2 cups (500 ml) sugar
1 1/2 cups (375 ml) unsalted butter
4 eggs
1 tsp (5 ml) soda
1 tsp (5 ml) milk
2 tsp (10 ml) baking powder
1 cup (250 ml) milk
3 cups (750 ml) flour
1 tsp (5 ml) vanilla
2 tbsp (60 ml) dark cocoa

For Chocolate Glaze
10 oz (300 g) milk chocolate
3.5 oz (100 g) dark chocolate
1 tbsp (15 ml) vegetable shortening
pinch salt
1 cup (250 ml) boiling water
1 tbsp (15 ml) cornstarch
1 tsp (5 ml) vanilla

Blend sugar and butter together. Beat eggs together, blend in. Dissolve soda in milk, stir into mixture. Add remaining ingredients, blend together. Place in 12-inch (30-cm) round pan, bake 45 minutes at 350°F (175°C).

For glaze, mix chocolate, shortening, and salt in boiling water. Cook in small pot on stovetop. Wet cornstarch in 2 tbsp (30 ml) cold water, stir well. Add to chocolate mix, blend well. Cook until thick. Remove from heat, add vanilla. Cool in fridge. Spread glaze over cake when glaze and cake are both cool.

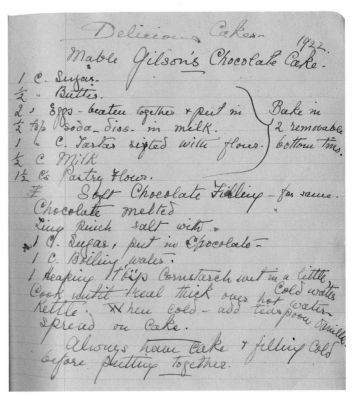

Mable Gilson's Chocolate Cake, 1922

CEDAR-PLANKED MACKEREL WITH PARSLEY MASHED POTATOES

Serves 2

For Mashed Potatoes
2 medium russet potatoes
2–3 tbsp (30–45 ml) whole milk or cream
1–2 tbsp (15–30 ml) butter
salt, pepper, to taste
2 tbsp (30 ml) chopped parsley
pinch nutmeg
1 egg

For Fish
1 fresh mackerel, cut into 2 fillets
1–2 tbsp (15–30 ml) olive oil, plus more
  for the plank
3 crushed juniper berries
1/2 lemon, zested and juiced (use
  vegetable peeler so it's thick)
4–6 sprigs thyme
salt, pepper, to taste

Soak plank in water at least 30 minutes.

Peel, rinse, cut, and boil potatoes in salted water. Drain in colander, let steam 2 minutes. In same pot, combine milk, butter, salt, pepper, parsley, and nutmeg. Heat over medium heat until butter is melted and milk is warm.

Add potatoes, mash until smooth. Adjust seasoning with salt and pepper. Add egg, mix thoroughly. Put potatoes in piping bag with star or round tip.

Pat mackerel dry with paper towel. Mix oil, lemon juice, zest, juniper berries, and thyme in medium bowl. Dip mackerel in mixture.

Brush olive oil on plank, place fish on it, skin side down. Ensure that lemon zest and thyme are on both sides of fish. Pipe potatoes around fish in desired pattern. Bake at 375°F (190°C) 20 to 25 minutes, or until fish is tender. (If needed, place pan under rack to catch drippings.) Carefully remove plank from oven and serve.

If cooking on BBQ, use low flame. Recipe also works well for salmon, haddock, and char.

"It's almost impossible to find shad, and it's so bony. I went with mackerel, as mackerel and shad have a close relationship. I was just thinking of the flavours I'd like to see with the fish; juniper gives oily fish a unique flavour. And juniper is an old-world flavour."

BEN KELLY, KITCHEN DOOR CATERING

Planked Shad With Potato

Have the fish split as for broiling, rinse quickly in cold water and dry thoroughly. Heat the plank in the oven, brush over with vegetable oil and lay the fish that has been dusted with salt and paprika on it. Fasten securely, pour over a little melted butter or oleo and bake in a hot oven for twenty-five minutes. Then brush again with melted shortening and arrange a border of creamy seasoned mashed potatoes around the edge of the plank. Brush this over with beaten egg and run under the broiler of the gas range for five or six minutes. Garnish with radish roses, small stuffed green peppers and slices of lemon dipped in chopped parsley.

Planked Shad with Potato, 1922

UNIACKE ESTATE MUSEUM PARK

SCALLOPED CLAMS

Serves 6

36 fresh, local clams in the shell
2 cups (500 ml) cracker crumbs
1/2 tsp (2 ml) salt
1/8 tsp (1 ml) pepper
1/4 cup (60 ml) butter or margarine,
   melted
1/4 tsp (1/2 ml) Worcestershire sauce
1 cup (250 ml) clam liquor
milk, as needed to top up clam liquor

Wash clams thoroughly under cold running water. Shuck, reserve liquor. Chop clams.

In mixing bowl, combine crumbs, salt, pepper, and butter. Sprinkle third of crumb mixture in greased 1-quart (1-litre) baking dish. Cover with half clams. Repeat layers. Add Worcestershire sauce and milk to liquor, pour over casserole. Bake at 350°F (175°C) 30 minutes or until brown.

Delicate clams, with their taste of the sea, have long been part of the great bounty found on Nova Scotia shores.

"It calls for bread crumbs in it, so I wanted to stay with that. It was a simple recipe; I figured everyone was getting back from the war and there wasn't much. I treated it as a casserole and baked it in the oven."

CHRIS BOLT, THE PRESS GANG

SCALLOPED CLAMS

12 clams chopped put in well-buttered dish alternate layers of clams. Sliced raw potatoes with a little onion, salt, pepper and butter. Put layer of crumbs on top pour on liquor from clams fill dish with milk and bake two hours.

Scalloped Clams, 1922

ROASTED TOMATO SOUP

Serves 4

10–12 Roma tomatoes
salt, pepper, to taste
2–3 tbsp (30–45 ml) olive oil
1 medium onion, medium diced
2 medium cloves garlic, sliced
1 cup (250 ml) whipping cream
3 cups (750 ml) whole milk
1–2 tbsp (15–30 ml) sugar
salt, pepper, to taste
8–10 large basil leaves

Slice tomatoes in half lengthwise, place on baking sheet, cut side up. Drizzle with olive oil, season with salt and pepper. Roast at 400°F (204°C) 60 minutes, or until edges start to blacken. Remove from oven, set aside.

Heat medium pot over medium-high heat. Add remaining olive oil and onions. Sauté onions 2 to 4 minutes, or until they start to brown. Add garlic, stir constantly 1 to 2 minutes. Just before garlic starts to colour, add tomatoes, stir 2 minutes. Add cream, milk, and sugar. Heat through, season with salt and pepper, add basil.

Purée soup with immersion blender or in stand blender. If using stand blender, take centrepiece out of lid and cover with tea towel (to prevent pressure popping off lid). Once puréed, season with sugar, salt, and pepper.

"The handwriting puts the recipe in a more human context. It adds an element of mystery as you imagine the person who took the time to write this recipe down. What was going on in the world? What did this recipe mean to them? Who did they cook it for? Who was Mrs. Frampton? A neighbour, a mother in-law, a family friend? I roasted tomatoes for sweetened flavour so I wouldn't have to add too much sugar. People prefer lighter dishes now."

BEN KELLY, KITCHEN DOOR CATERING

Mrs. Framptons Tomato Soup, 1922

INDIAN CURRY SOUP

Serves 4

2 tbsp (30 ml) ghee
1 yellow onion, minced
1 medium carrot, minced
1 pound (450 g) boneless, skinless
chicken breasts, cubed
2 garlic cloves, minced
1 tbsp (15 ml) + 1 tsp (5 ml) curry powder
2 cups (500 ml) chicken broth
1 1/2 cups (350-ml can) full fat
coconut milk
1 tbsp (15 ml) honey
salt, pepper, to taste
1 green apple, diced
lime wedges
chopped cilantro, for garnish

Place large pot over medium heat. Add ghee, onion, and carrot. Sauté until onion becomes translucent, at least 5 minutes. Add in chicken and garlic, cook chicken until it's no longer pink, about 7 to 8 minutes. Add curry powder, mix to cook about 3 minutes.

Add broth, coconut milk, honey, salt, pepper, and green apple. Mix to combine, then let simmer 10 to 15 minutes, until mixture has reduced by one-third. To serve, squeeze fresh lime juice and garnish with cilantro.

"I love curries and that stuff, so I thought this was great. Spices were almost used as currency in the past. I was surprised curry was even used then. British soldiers must have bought it."

CHRIS BOLT, THE PRESS GANG

MULLIGATAWNY SOUP

Five cups white stock.
1 cup tomatoes.
¼ cup onion cut in slices.
¼ cup carrot cut in cubes.
¼ cup celery cut in cubes.
1 pepper, finely chopped.
1 apple sliced.
1 cup raw chicken cut in dice.
¼ cup butter.
1-3 cup flour.
1 teaspoon curry powder.
Blade of mace.
2 cloves.
Sprig of parsley.
Salt and pepper.

MRS. ALBRO ETTINGER.
229 North street.

Mulligatawny Soup, 1922

MEXICAN RAREBIT

Serves 4 to 6

3 tbsp (45 ml) unsalted butter

1 small onion, chopped

salt, pepper, to taste

2 cups (500 ml) shredded Chihuahua
   cheese

1/4 cup (60 ml) whole milk

1/2 cup (125 ml) Mexican pilsner-style
   beer, such as Pacifico

1 tbsp (15 ml) pickled jalapeño juice

1 tsp (5 ml) ground cumin

1 loaf cornbread

pickled jalapeño slices, for garnish

chopped tomato, for garnish

cilantro leaves, for garnish

Heat broiler to high, arrange rack about 5 inches (12 cm) away from heat. Melt butter in medium saucepan over medium heat. Add onions, season with salt and pepper. Cook, stirring occasionally, until golden and soft, about 10 minutes.

Add cheese, milk, and beer, cook until cheese is melted. Add pickle juice and cumin, stir until smooth. Remove from heat, season as needed. Cover to keep warm.

Slice cornbread into thick slices and place on a foil-lined baking sheet. Toast under broiler 2 to 3 minutes. Flip, cover each slice with cheese sauce. Return to broiler until cheese is golden, about 2 minutes more.

Top with pickled jalapeño slices, tomatoes, and cilantro. Serve immediately.

"I couldn't figure out why it was called rabbit and there was no rabbit in it. (The word rabbit was used before rarebit in the original Welsh dish). You wouldn't get away with that today; menus have to be so transparent. Common cheese was probably like a young mozzarella. We expanded on the flavour."

CHRIS BOLT, THE PRESS GANG

MEXICAN RABBIT

1 lb. common cheese.

2 eggs beaten lightly.

1 table spoon butter.

1 green pepper cut in squares.

2-3 cup canned corn pulp.

1-2 teaspoon paprika.

1-2 teaspoon salt.

2-3 cup tomato cut in pieces.

Melt the butter in it and cook green pepper until a little soft; add cheese cut in thin pieces and stir until melted, add corn pulp mixed with the seasonings and egg and stir until smooth, then add tomato and stir until hot throughout, serve at once on hot crackers.

MRS. G. R. RIPLEY,
45 Cork Street.

Mexican Rabbit, 1922

CUMBERLAND SAUCE

Yields 8 to 10 portions

1 tbsp (15 ml) minced onion
1 orange, zested and juiced
1/2 cup (125 ml) Nova Scotia blueberries
1/2 cup (125 ml) Nova Scotia red wine
1/2 cup (125 ml) sugar
1 jar Galloping Cows wild blueberry
   pepper jelly
1/2 tsp (2 ml) salt

Combine all ingredients in saucepan, bring to simmer, cook 10 minutes.

Serve warm or cool with Nova Scotia pork.

"Cumberland sauce was really old school; you wouldn't see it outside of Great Britain. They are still serving it with ham. This is a Nova Scotia riff on that—we have blueberries, and maple, and red wine. With the blueberry jelly the sauce is quite delicious. I haven't made Cumberland sauce for twenty-five years since cooking school! It was everywhere on restaurant menus in the '40s and '50s."

ALAN CROSBY, WHITE POINT BEACH RESORT

CUMBERLAND DRESSING

Currant jelly, salt, pepper, White Vinegar and olive oil. To a teaspoon of currant jelly add 1 tablespoon of vinegar, a pinch of salt and pepper and 3 tablespoons of oil.

Cumberland Dressing, c .1930s

UNIACKE ESTATE MUSEUM PARK

COUNTRY CLUB BACON AND EGGS

Serves 6

12 slices bread, crusts removed
18 oz (1/2 kilo) sharp cheddar cheese,
  grated
18 oz (1/2 kilo) Swiss cheese, grated
1 lb (450 g) Canadian bacon, thinly sliced
6 eggs, beaten
3 cups (750 ml) milk
1/2 tsp (2 ml) salt
fresh chives, for garnish

Alternate layers of bread slices, cheeses, and bacon in 7- x 11-inch (17- x 28-cm) baking pan until all are used. Beat eggs with milk and salt in bowl. Pour over casserole. Cover. Refrigerate overnight. Bake at 325°F (160°C) 50 to 60 minutes. Cut into equal portions, serve with chopped chives.

"A strange one with the hard-boiled eggs. It was not the era of cuisine but I can imagine hard-working people eating this and having a nap after. We were trying to flavour it; we put pretty much everything on the breakfast table into the casserole dish. It's filling and delicious."

CHRIS BOLT, THE PRESS GANG

COUNTRY CLUB EGGS.

1 medium onion, chopped.
2 tbsp. butter.
2 tbsp. flour.
6 eggs, hardboiled.
1 canned pimento, shredded.
1/2 tsp. salt.
1 1/2 cups Farmers' milk.

1-8 tsp. pepper.
Dash of paprika.
1/2 cup grated cheese.
1 tsp. parsley, chopped.
2 egg yolks, beaten, with
2 tbsp. cold milk.
Juice of 1/2 a lemon.

Cook onions in the butter until tender but not brown, then add flour and stir to a smooth paste. Pour in the milk and simmer till sauce is thickened. Add eggs, sliced pimento, salt, pepper, paprika, grated cheese, parsley and the egg yolks beaten with the milk. Simmer for 2 or 3 minutes. Just before serving stir in lemon juice. Serve on hot saltines, on toast points, or in croustades. Serves six.

Country Club Eggs, c. 1936

MEAT LOAF WITH BACON

Serves 4 to 6

1 tbsp (15 ml) olive oil
1 onion, chopped
1 large celery stalk, chopped
2 garlic cloves, minced
1 jalapeño pepper, chopped with seeds
2 tsp (10 ml) kosher salt
1/2 tsp (2 ml) ground cumin
1/4 tsp (1 ml) ground nutmeg
2 eggs
1/2 cup (125 ml) milk
1/2 cup (125 ml) tomato sauce or ketchup
1 cup (250 ml) dry bread crumbs
1 lb (450 g) lean ground beef
1/2 lb (225 g) ground pork
1/2 lb (225 g) ground veal or lamb
4 strips thick-sliced bacon

Heat oven to 350°F (175°C). Heat oil in medium skillet, over medium heat, with onion, celery, garlic, and jalapeño. Cook until vegetables are tender but not browned, about 10 minutes. Add salt, cumin, and nutmeg. Remove from heat. In large bowl, whisk eggs, then blend in milk, tomato sauce, and bread crumbs. Add meat and cooked vegetables, stir or use hands to combine. Pat into 9- x 5-inch (23- x 12-cm) loaf pan.

Cut bacon strips in half, place over loaf, tucking ends in. Bake 75 minutes or until thermometer registers 150°F (65°C). Remove from oven, pour off fat. Let stand 10 minutes before serving.

"I had to make the original recipe to see what things I was going to change. It was pretty bland but it is survival food. Not to be a snob, but it's just to fill you up. We put thick-sliced bacon over top so bacon fat dripped down into the bread to give it more flavour. The end result was really gorgeous."

CHRIS BOLT, THE PRESS GANG

MAYFLOWER MEAT LOAF.
1 lb. beef, ground.
2 tbsp. butter.
1 egg.
1 cup cracker crumbs.
1 tsp. salt.
1/4 tsp. pepper.
2 slices bacon.
1 cup Farmers' milk.
Combine meat with other ingredients, using enough milk so that mixture holds well together. Form into loaf, in covered baking pan. Lay slices bacon across top. Bake covered 1½ hours in moderate oven (375 F.). Uncover last half-hour to brown. Serves eight.

Mayflower Meat Loaf, c. 1936

WARTIME ECONOMY BOOK
OF RECIPES FOR 1945

Selected From More Than 8000 Maritime Recipes

This supplement is presented to our readers as a helpful wartime service, to promote economy, nutrition and efficiency. The tempting and interesting recipes in this thirty-two page supplement have been selected from the thousands submitted in the recent contest conducted by The Halifax Herald and The Halifax Mail. The photograph below is an actual picture of the great pile of entries, more than 8000 in all, sent in by readers of these papers. They came from over 300 different communities in Nova Scotia and Prince Edward Island, as well as some from New Brunswick.

Chapter 5

THE WAR YEARS AND AFTER

The Wartime Economy Book of Recipes was published by the *Halifax Herald and* the *Halifax Mail* in 1945 as "a helpful wartime service to promote economy, nutrition and efficiency." The paper held a contest attracting over eight thousand recipes from throughout the Maritimes, from which they filled thirty-two pages. Citizens submitted their ideas to survive the harsh war years, such as saving butter by adding gelatin and milk, stretching sugar by dissolving it in water and tartaric acid, and greasing baking dishes with bacon fat. This chapter includes recipes from that publication as well as the *Grand-Pre Cook Book, Kitchen Army Nutrition and Receipt Book*, and Atlantic War Fund Club Halifax's *Favourite Recipes*.

Also featured here are popular Acadian recipes from the d'Entremont family's collection. African Nova Scotia recipes are from *The Clarion—for Church and Community*, a newspaper first published in 1946 and edited by esteemed human rights activist, New Glasgow-born Carrie Best.

Facing page: Published by the *Halifax Herald* and the *Halifax Mail*, this supplement was compiled from more than 8,000 recipes, from more than 300 communities, submitted to the newspapers' contest. (Nova Scotia Archives) MG 100 vol. 126 no. 12

LAVENDER CREAM EARL-GREY-INFUSED BLUEBERRY MUFFINS

Yields 1 dozen muffins

3/4 cup (175 ml) unsalted butter
1 tbsp (15 ml) Tea Brewery lavender
    cream Earl Grey
1 cup (250 ml) Acadian maple syrup
1 whole egg
2 egg whites
1 tsp (5 ml) vanilla bean paste
3/4 cup (175 ml) milk
2 cups (500 ml) all-purpose flour
1 tsp (5 ml) baking powder
1/4 tsp (1 ml) baking soda
1/2 tsp (2 ml) salt
1 1/2 (375 ml) cups local blueberries,
    fresh or frozen

Melt butter in saucepan with loose tea. Allow to simmer 5 minutes, remove from heat.

Once it has cooled slightly, pour through strainer to remove tea.

In mixer, combine maple syrup and butter. Add egg, egg whites, and vanilla bean paste. Mix well, add milk.

In separate bowl, combine flour, baking powder, baking soda, and salt.

Add dry ingredients to liquid, mix until combined. Gently fold in blueberries.

Scoop batter into lined or well-greased muffin pan and bake at 350°F (175°C) 20 to 25 minutes, or until wooden skewer inserted into centre comes out clean.

"The original recipe was very simple and wasn't very sweet. I changed the fat as I don't like to use shortening in my recipes. Butter is my choice here—not just for the great flavour, but it's excellent to use when infusing tea into a recipe. There's a reason blueberry muffins are still so popular today. They're delicious, and in Nova Scotia sourcing them locally is easy!"

VANESSA MacDONALD, FIRESIDE KITCHEN

BLUEBERRY MUFFINS

2 cups of flour
4 tablespoons sugar
4 teaspoons baking powder
½ teaspoon salt

1 egg, well beaten
1 cup of milk
4 tablespoons melted shortening
1 cup of berries

Sift dry ingredients, add blueberries, combine egg, milk and shortening; turn into dry ingredients, stir just enough to combine, fill greased muffin tins two-thirds full and bake about 20 minutes in a hot oven.

Blueberry Muffins, 1939

HALIBURTON HOUSE MUSEUM

ANGELS ON HORSEBACK

Take as many oysters as required, put each one into piece of fat bacon and fasten. Place under grille until oyster swells and bacon is cooked. They should be turned whilst cooking to ensure bacon is done evenly.

- Mrs. Courtney.

Angels on Horseback, 1940

ROSS FARM MUSEUM

FRIED OYSTER PO' BOY

Serves 4

For Corn Relish
1 cup (250 ml) fresh corn kernels
   (if frozen, thaw first)
2/3 cup (160 ml) sweet onions, diced
1 tbsp (15 ml) sweet bell peppers, diced
1 tsp (5 ml) jalapeño peppers, minced
1/3 cup (80 ml) cider vinegar
1 1/2 tbsp (22 ml) granulated sugar
1 pinch kosher salt
1/2 tsp (2 ml) dry mustard
1/2 tsp (2 ml) mustard seed
1/8 tsp (1 ml) celery seed

For Oysters
1 cup (250 ml) flour
1 cup (250 ml) cornmeal
1 tbsp (15 ml) onion powder
1 tbsp (15 ml) garlic powder
12 oysters
salt, pepper, to taste

For Cilantro Aioli
1 cup (250 ml) mayo
1/2 bunch cilantro, finely chopped
1 clove garlic, finely chopped
1/2 lime, juiced

12 slider buns
12 strips bacon, fried until crispy
onion sprouts

For corn relish, combine all ingredients in large stockpot. Bring to boil over medium-high heat. Reduce heat to low, simmer another 15 minutes.

For oysters, mix flour, cornmeal, onion and garlic powders. Dredge oysters, fry at 350°F (175°C) until golden brown.

For cilantro aioli, combine mayo, cilantro, garlic, and lime in bowl. Spread aioli on both halves of slider buns. Add onion sprouts, 2 strips bacon, and 2 fried oysters on each. Top with spicy corn relish.

"I didn't know they prepared oysters in that way. I thought if you bread and fry them, wouldn't they be great as a po' boy slider? It's a modern twist on an old recipe."

TAMMY MCKEARNEY, LANE'S PRIVATEER INN

MAPLE AND SPICED RUM PARFAIT TRUFFLES

Yields 18 to 20 truffles

1 cup (250 ml) whipping cream
1/3 cup (75 ml) Nova Scotia maple syrup
3 tbsp (45 ml) J.D. Shore spiced rum
5 egg yolks
1 tsp (5 ml) cinnamon
4 oatcakes or preferred cookies, crushed
1/2 cup (125 ml) Just Us dark chocolate

"I have never made a parfait before and it wasn't what I expected. It wasn't bad; the original recipe works. I don't know why more people don't make a parfait; it's extremely versatile when it comes to flavour, super easy, and quick— especially compared to ice cream as no fancy equipment is required. We rolled it up into balls, covered it with oatcake crumbs, and dipped it in chocolate like a mini-ice-cream sandwich. I'll keep making it as it is so delicious."

VANESSA MacDONALD, FIRESIDE KITCHEN

In mixer, whip cream to soft peaks, cover, set aside, and refrigerate.

Cook maple syrup and rum over medium-high heat in heavy-bottomed saucepan until syrup reaches soft-ball stage, about 5 minutes or 235°F (112°C) on candy thermometer.

As syrup is cooking, beat egg yolks and cinnamon on high until it thickens and forms ribbons when beater is lifted. Once syrup is ready, decrease mixer speed to low, slowly add syrup to beaten egg yolks. Increase speed to high, beat mixture until thickened and cooled.

Fold in whipping cream, pour into freezer-safe, air-tight container. Freeze at least 6 hours.

When parfait is ready, place crushed oatcakes into bowl. Melt chocolate in small pot.

Scoop parfait with small ice-cream or cookie-dough scoop. Roll parfait in crushed oatcakes, dip upper half into chocolate, and return to freezer. Repeat with each scoop.

Serve for dessert, or even bite-size for entertaining.

This recipe is an excellent way to enjoy the pure, wonderful flavour of Nova Scotia maple syrup.

(Facing page) A fresh-faced boy poses with Hamilton's cookies in 1941 in wartime Halifax. (E. A. Bollinger, Nova Scotia Archives, accession no. 1975-305 1941 no 319 e)

MAPLE PARFAIT

4 eggs
2/3 cup hot maple syrup
1 pt. whipping cream

        Beat eggs slightly and pour on syrup. **Stir**
and cook in double boiler until mixture thickens, cool and
add cream beaten very stiff - Add pinch of salt when cooking.
Freeze.

        - Mrs. Oxner

Maple Parfait, 1940

GINGER-ALE SNAPS

Yields 2 dozen cookies

2 cups (500 ml) local dark stout, such as
    Saltbox Brewing Co's Old Foundry stout
1/4 cup (60 ml) Cosman & Whidden honey
3/4 cup (175 ml) unsalted butter
1 1/4 cups (300 ml) brown sugar
1 egg
1/2 tsp (2 ml) vanilla
2 cups (500 ml) all-purpose flour
1 tsp (5 ml) baking soda
1/4 tsp (1 ml) salt
1 1/2 tsp (7 ml) ground cloves
1/2 tsp (2 ml) ground nutmeg
1/2 tsp (2 ml) ginger
2 tsp (10 ml) cinnamon
1 orange, zested
1 cup (250 ml) candied ginger
1/4 cup (60 ml) white sugar, for rolling
1/4 cup (60 ml) icing sugar, for rolling

Cook stout and honey in saucepan over medium heat, stirring occasionally until liquid reduces to about 1/3 cup (75 ml) syrup. Remove from heat and let cool.

In mixer, cream butter and sugar. Add egg and vanilla. In separate mixing bowl, combine flour, soda, salt, cloves, nutmeg, ginger, cinnamon, and zest. Add dry ingredients in thirds, alternating with stout syrup. Add candied ginger, mix just until evenly distributed.

Scoop dough, roll into balls. Roll in sugar, then icing sugar. This will create an extra-crispy shell.

Place on lined cookie sheet, bake at 350°F (175°C), or 325°F (160°C) in convection oven, 12 to 15 minutes.

"These are such a classic cookie. The original is simple and tasty, but I knew I could zest things up. I didn't use molasses; it can easily be substituted out for local maple syrup or honey. What else can we put in a gingersnap that's local? Beer! It adds fantastic flavour and colour to the cookie."

VANESSA MacDONALD, FIRESIDE KITCHEN

GINGER SNAPS

Sift together 3 cups flour
1 heaping teaspoon soda
2 teaspoons ginger
1 teaspoon salt

Blend in 1 cup butter or any shortening.
Then mix in a little more than 1 cup of molasses chill.
Roll thin. Bake in a moderate oven.

                       - Mrs. Norman Stanbury.

Ginger Snaps, 1940

HALIBURTON HOUSE MUSEUM

THREE-IN-ONE ROLLS

Yields 48 rolls

For Soaker
1/3 cup (75 ml) Speerville 12-grain cereal
1/3 cup (75 ml) hot water

For Yeast
1 cup (250 ml) warm water
1 cup (250 ml) lukewarm milk
2 tbsp (30 ml) butter, melted
2 packages active dry yeast
  (4 1/2 tsp or 22 ml)
1 tbsp (15 ml) local honey

For First Flour Mix
1 cup (250 ml) all-purpose flour
1/2 cup (125 ml) whole wheat flour
1 tsp (5 ml) salt

For Second Flour Mix
3/4 cup (175 ml) all-purpose flour
3/4 cup (175 ml) Kamut flour
1 tsp (5 ml) turmeric
1 tsp (5 ml) salt
1/4 cup (60 ml) squash, cooked and mashed

For Third Flour Mix
1 3/4 cup (300 ml) all-purpose flour
1 tsp (5 ml) salt

To make soaker, mix cereal with hot water in medium-sized bowl. Set aside.

In another bowl, mix warm water, milk, melted butter, yeast, and honey. Let sit 3 minutes or until yeast is dissolved.

Mix first amount of flours and salt with soaker. Set aside. In second bowl, mix second flour amount with turmeric, salt, and squash. Set aside. In third bowl, mix third amount of flour and salt.

Mix yeast mixture until smooth. Divide evenly between the 3 bowls and mix each with spoon until shaggy dough forms. Knead each on floured surface until smooth, about 5 to 6 minutes (or 2 to 3 minutes in stand mixer). Place dough in separate greased bowls, cover with wrap, and let rise until double.

Punch down dough and divide each into 16 pieces. Cover to prevent drying out. Roll each piece into 8-inch- (20-cm-) long strand. Roll each strand of multigrain dough over damp tea towel, then roll in 12-grain cereal. Roll each strand of white dough in mixture of summer savory, olive oil, and garlic salt.

Braid together one strand from each type of dough, tucking in the ends. Place on baking sheet lined with parchment. Repeat. Cover and let rise until almost double.

Mix egg with water, brush over braids. Bake in 400°F (204°C) oven 12 to 15 minutes or until lightly golden.

Toppings

1/2 cup (125 ml) Speerville 12-grain
   cereal

2 tbsp (30 ml) summer savory

1/2 cup (125 ml) olive oil

1 tsp (5 ml) garlic salt

For Egg Wash

1 egg, beaten

1 tbsp (15 ml) water

"My mother made a cloverleaf roll growing up, but I had never heard of 3 in 1. I didn't know what to make of it, to be honest. I get that it was what people had available in their pantry, and a way to make a dinner roll fancier. As a boulanger/baker by trade, I felt I could go someplace really fun and creative with this."

VANESSA MacDONALD, FIRESIDE KITCHEN

Three-In-One Rolls, 1943

46   THREE-IN-ONE ROLLS

1 yeast	2 c. warm water
½ c. sugar	1½ t. salt
2 beaten eggs	1|3 c. melted shortening
3 c. white flour	1 c. white flour
1 c. whole wheat flour	1 c. yellow corn meal

Soften yeast in luke warm water; add sugar, salt, shortening and eggs. Add 3 c. white flour. Beat light. Divide into three equal parts. Add 1 c. flour to first part; kneed until smooth on lightly floured board. Add whole wheat flour to second part; knead smooth. Add corn meal to third part; kneed smooth. Place in separate greased bowls; grease top of dough; cover and let rise until double in bulk, about 1 hr cut down; let rise again until double. Shape in balls. Put one ball of each type of dough into each greased muffin pan. Cover and let rise until double in bulk. Brush with shortening. Bake in hot oven (425°F.) 15 minutes.

Almost any stew is, we think, improved by cooking on the day before it is to be used; and for a time-saver, why not double the quantities, serve stew one day (maybe with dumplings, hot biscuits, macaroni or spaghetti or rice, as a border). . . and reheat the remainder a couple of days later, for turning into the paste-lined casserole to make a meat-pie.

¾ pound beef kidney	Boiling water
1½ lbs. round steak	6 small potatoes
Seasoned flour	6 small whole carrots
Hot shortening or dripping	Pie paste
2 tblsp. (or more) finely-chopped onion	

Soak the kidney in salted cold water for 1 hour. Drain and cut in sections. Dice the steak. Coat kidney and steak pieces with seasoned flour and brown well in a little hot shortening or dripping, with the onion. Cover well with boiling water; bring to boil, lower heat and simmer for 1½ hours. (Of course, if you have a deep-well cooker, this is a grand time to use it.) Add potatoes and carrots, add water if necessary to cover again, and season with salt, pepper and Worcestershire sauce. Cover and simmer until meat and vegetables are tender. Thicken the liquid with flour, blended to smooth pouring consistency with cold water; season well.

Line the sides of a deep baking dish with pie-paste. Turn in the meat, vegetables and sauce. If you like, a support may be put in the dish before, turning in the stew, this keeps the crust from sinking. Cover pie with paste, in which eyelets have been cut for the escape of steam. Bake in a hot oven, 425° about 30 minutes.

Beefsteak and Kidney Pie, 1943

STEAK AND KIDNEY PIE

5–6 lamb kidneys
milk, to cover kidneys
1/2 cup (125 ml) flour, seasoned with
  salt and pepper
3 tbsp (45 ml) oil
1 lb (450 g) inside round, cubed
1 carrot, chopped
1 medium onion, sliced thinly
1 celery stalk, chopped
6–8 button mushrooms, cut in 4
1 tbsp (15 ml) tomato paste
1 cup (250 ml) local red wine
1 bay leaf
salt, pepper, to taste
4 cups (1 litre) beef stock, approx
2 medium russet potatoes, washed,
peeled, and diced
1 sprig rosemary
2–4 sprigs thyme
1 batch pie dough or puff pastry
1 egg, beaten
coarse salt, for sprinkling

*"I soaked the kidney in milk
to make it more acceptable to
modern palates, added more
vegetables, and made more like
a steak and kidney bourguignon.
It was really good; everyone at
the photo shoot ate it!"*

BEN KELLY, KITCHEN DOOR CATERING

Soak kidneys in milk overnight, or at least 2 hours.
Slice in 4, toss in seasoned flour. Shake off excess flour.
In medium-hot pan, sear kidneys in oil until lightly
browned, 2 to 3 minutes per side. Remove, set on paper
towel.

Toss beef in flour, shake off excess, brown on all sides.
Remove from pan, add carrot, onion, and celery. Cook,
stirring occasionally 3 to 4 minutes or until onions are
translucent. Add mushrooms. Cook, stirring regularly,
another 2 minutes. Add tomato paste, stir 1 minute.
Deglaze pan with wine, reduce by half.

Return beef, with juices, to pan. Return kidneys to pan
without juices. Add bay leaf, salt, pepper, and beef stock
to cover. Bring to boil, reduce heat to low, and simmer
uncovered 45 to 60 minutes. Add potatoes and herbs,
cook another 30 minutes. Adjust seasoning, remove
from heat, pick out stems from herbs.

Line pie plate or cast-iron pan with pie or puff pastry.
Ladle stew into pie crust. Brush edges with egg. Cover
with second sheet of pastry. Trim edges, pinch to seal.
Brush top with remaining egg, sprinkle with coarse salt.
Using knife tip, poke few holes to release steam.

Bake at 425°F (218°C) 35 to 45 minutes. Crust should be
golden brown and stew bubbling slightly out of steam
holes. Let sit at least 10 minutes at room temperature
before cutting.

PRESERVES BLUEBERRY BUCKLE

Yields 1 cake

For Base
1/2 cup (125 ml) unsalted butter, softened
1/2 cup (125 ml) caster sugar
1 egg
2 cups (500 ml) dark rye flour
2 1/2 tsp (14 ml) baking powder
1/2 tsp (2 ml) sea salt
1/4 tsp (1 ml) ground cinnamon
1/2 cup (125 ml) whole milk
1/4 tsp (1 ml) vanilla bean paste
1/2 cup (125 ml) Helen B's blueberry jam
1/2 cup (125 ml) Galloping Cows wild
   blueberry pepper spread

For Crumb Topping
1/2 cup (125 ml) caster sugar
1/2 cup (125 ml) flour, dark rye
1/2 cup (125 ml) Terra Beata Farms
   dried blueberries
1/4 cup (60 ml) unsalted butter, firm
   and cubed
1/2 tsp (2 ml) ground cinnamon

Preheat oven to 350°F (175°C). In electric stand mixture, speed 5, cream together butter and sugar, then add egg. In bowl, sift together flour, baking powder, salt, and cinnamon. Add milk, vanilla bean paste, and creamed mixture. Fold to form thick batter. Place batter into greased 10-inch (25-cm) cast-iron pan. Spread evenly. In bowl, whisk together jam and jelly. Spread over top. Then, using spoon handle, swirl mixture into batter.

In separate bowl, place crumb topping ingredients. Using your hands, incorporate butter until mealy mixture is formed (butter pieces the size of green peas). Evenly distribute topping over batter in cast-iron pan. Place in middle of oven, bake 1 hour and 45 minutes. Place on cooling rack to cool before serving.

"I look at buckle and it's made in summer months when blueberries are in peak season. What do I have available without going beyond local suppliers? We have to be aware of short growing seasons and of products available. I put a modern spin on these recipes without changing them too much."

T. J. PITTMAN, OLD FISH FACTORY RESTAURANT

Blueberry Buckle, 1943

---

15   **BLUEBERRY BUCKLE**

Cream thoroughly ½ c. shortening and ½ c. sugar; add 1 beaten egg and mix well. Sift 2 c. flour, ¼ t. salt, and 2½ t. baking powder; add to creamed mixture alternately with ½ c. milk. Pour into greased 8 in. layer cake pan and sprinkle 2 c. fresh blueberries over batter. Mix ½ c. sugar, ½ c. flour, ½ t. cinnamon and ¼ c. butter until crumbly; sprinkle over blueberries. Bake in moderate oven (350) 1 hour and 15 min. Cut in wedges and serve hot as dessert.

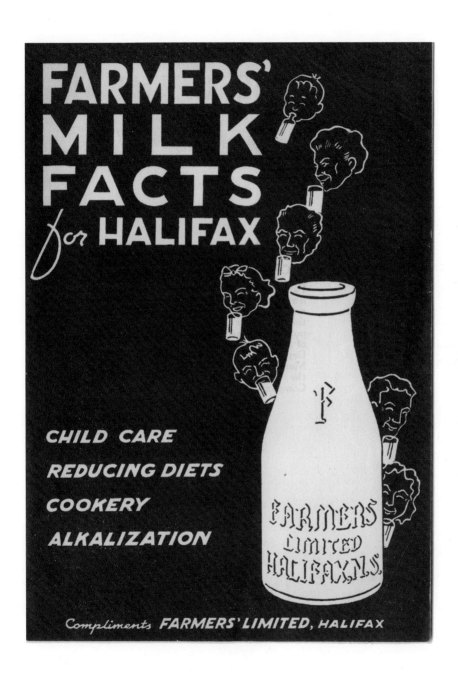

Farmers' Milk Facts for Halifax by Farmers' Limited, Halifax
(Nova Scotia Museum 84.92.14)

WHOLE WHEAT CRANBERRY BREAD

Yields 2 loaves

2 medium oranges, washed and quartered
1 cup (250 ml) butter, melted
3 eggs
1/3 cup (75 ml) orange juice
2 cups (500 ml) all-purpose flour
1 cup (250 ml) whole wheat flour
1/2 cup (125 ml) milled Nova Scotia
   flax seeds
2 tbsp (30 ml) baking powder
2 tsp (10 ml) salt
1 1/2 cups (375 ml) sugar
1 1/2 cups (375 ml) fresh or frozen
   cranberries
1/2 cup (125 ml) Terra Beata dried
   cranberries

Purée oranges in food processor, skin, seeds, and all! In large bowl, beat together butter, eggs, orange juice, and oranges. In medium bowl, combine dry ingredients. Mix wet and dry ingredients until just combined. Stir in cranberries.

Divide mix between 2 buttered loaf pans. Bake at 350°F (175°C) about 45 to 60 minutes until centre springs back. Cool slightly, remove from pans.

"The way they created the bread was to take a package of shredded wheat cereal. And it didn't include whole wheat flour. They probably didn't have such a thing; the whole refined white flour was becoming in vogue. My loaf utilizes whole oranges—just wash the oranges and take the stickers off. It's a wonderful way to make a quasi-nutritious version of a muffin. The loaf itself is quite dense, full of goodness."

ALAN CROSBY, WHITE POINT BEACH RESORT

WHOLE WHEAT CRANBERRY LOAF

2 cups once-sifted all-purpose flour
or 2¼ cups once-sifted pastry flour
5 teas. baking powder
¾ teas. salt
2|3 cup granulated sugar

1 cup crushed shredded wheat
1½ cups chopped raw cranberries
1 egg
2|3 cup milk
1|3 cup melted shortening or butter

    Measure flour and sift with baking powder, salt and sugar. Add the shred,
ded wheat, cranberries and nutmeats. Beat the egg until very light and ad-
mill and melted fat. Turn the liquid ingredients into the dry mixture and com
bine well. Spread in a greased and floured loaf pan and bake in moderate oven-
350°, for 50 to 60 minutes.

Whole Wheat Cranberry Loaf, 1943

RED WINE CRANBERRY JELLIED SALAD WITH CRANBERRY AIOLI

Serves 8 to 10

For Jellied Salad
3 cups (750 ml) fresh or frozen Nova
   Scotia cranberries
1 cup (250 ml) local red wine, such as
   Leon Millot
1 cup (250 ml) Terra Beata pure
   cranberry juice
1 orange, zested
1 tsp (5 ml) dry thyme or few sprigs fresh
1 1/4 cups (300 ml) sugar
2 tbsp (30 ml) gelatin
1/4 cup (60 ml) cold water

For Cranberry Aioli
1 tbsp (15 ml) butter
1/2 cup (125 ml) fine dice onion
1/4 tsp (1 ml) dry thyme
1/4 tsp (1 ml) ground black pepper
juice of denuded (zested) orange
reserved cranberry pulp
1/4 tsp (1 ml) salt
1 tsp (5 ml) sugar
1/2 cup (125 ml) mayonnaise
1/4 cup (60 ml) orange juice

In medium pot, combine all salad ingredients, except gelatin and water, bring to boil. Simmer over reduced heat just until berries are set to pop. Strain mixture through fine sieve, pressing to extract all goodness. Reserve pulp. About 3 cups (750 ml) liquid remain.

Dissolve gelatin in water. Stir into berry mix, combine well. Pour mixture into prepared mold of your choice.

Chill 3 to 4 hours.

Briefly dip exterior of mold in hot-water bath. Invert on prepared platter.

For aioli, melt butter in small frying pan, cook onions until tender. Add thyme, pepper, and orange juice from zested orange. Add cranberry pulp, salt, and sugar, cook 1 minute. Remove from heat, stir in mayo. Transfer mix to blender jar, blend in second orange juice amount until smooth.

This celebration of the beauty and taste of local cranberries provides the perfect side to Nova Scotia pork schnitzel or roast turkey.

"Everything old is new again. Does this bring you back? In this updated version we've added Nova Scotia wine and local cranberries. However in homage to our more frugal ancestors (my Mom), nothing goes to waste. We'll use the pulp from the cranberries and the denuded orange to boost our cranberry aioli."

ALAN CROSBY, WHITE POINT BEACH RESORT

Raw Cranberry Salad, 1943

24   **RAW CRANBERRY SALAD**

1 quart cranberries	1 cup chopped celery
1½ cups granulated sugar	1 cup diced unpeeled apples
2 tbsp. granulated gelatin	½ cup orange juice

Serves 8

Grind the cranberries in food chopper, using fine blade. Add sugar, mix, and let stand for 15 minutes, stirring occasionally. Soften the gelatin in the orange juice for five minutes, then stir over hot water until dissolved. Mix gelatin mixture with cranberries, celery, apples. Next place ingredients in individual molds which have first been rinsed in cold water. Chill in the refrigerator until set. In serving, unmold on crisp lettuce, plain or with a garnish of mayonnaise.

Cranberry Pickers, Clam Harbour, 1954
(Robert Norwood, Nova Scotia Archives,
accession no. 1987-481 envelope 1011-39)

CHAUDRÉE DE POISSON

Serves 4 to 6

2 tbsp (30 ml) butter

1/2 cup (125 ml) double smoked bacon, finely diced

1 medium onion, finely diced

2 carrots, peeled, finely diced

2 stalks celery, finely diced

1 tbsp (15 ml) fresh tarragon

4 cups (1 litre) fish stock

2 cups (500 ml) diced potato

1 1/2 cups (354-ml can) evaporated milk

3 large haddock filets, cut into 1-inch (2.5-cm) pieces

salt, pepper, to taste

Melt butter in soup pot, sauté bacon until it just starts to crisp. Set aside. Sauté onion, carrots, and celery in butter-bacon fat until soft. Add tarragon, fish stock, and potatoes; cook until potatoes are tender. Add reserved bacon, evaporated milk, and haddock, cook over medium low gently poaching the fish. Season with salt and pepper.

"The old recipe was very simple—fish and water and potato, and that was it. We gave it a different twist with tarragon and creamy butter and added carrots and different components. But we kept it as a traditional milk-type chowder. We wanted to stay true to Acadian chowder. Smoked bacon added a new dimension."

ALAIN BOSSE, THE KILTED CHEF

Isabelle
d'Entremont

Soupe au poisson
1 livre de poisson frais
1 morceau de lard salé (1/4 de livre à peu près)
coupé en petits morceaux
1/2 tasse d'oignon émincé
poivre et sel
4 tasses d'eau bouillante
1 1/2 tasses de pommes de terre hachées

frire le lard, ajouter l'oignon, remuer ensemble
ajouter le poisson, remuer ensemble
ajouter l'eau bouillante, les pommes de terre
Cuire à feu moyen, une trentaine de minutes
ou jusqu'à ce que les pommes de terre soient cuites

Soupe aux Poisson, pre-1945

HERBES SALÉES

Yields 1 cup

3 cups (750 ml) green onions, diced
1/2 cup (125 ml) carrots, thinly sliced and diced
2 tbsp (30 ml) fresh parsley, finely chopped
1/2 cup (125 ml) coarse salt
2 sprigs fresh thyme

Combine green onions, carrots, and parsley. Place one-quarter in bottom of large Mason jar, top with one quarter salt. Continue layering, finishing with salt. Slide thyme into side of jar for visual effect. Refrigerate up to 2 months.

"These recipes are very Acadian; there was not a household that didn't have herbes salées in the refrigerator to add to a casserole or fricot. It was a commonly used item. Salt and pepper was the main seasoning. We added parsley, carrots, and a few sprigs of thyme to make it more modern."

ALAIN BOSSE, THE KILTED CHEF

Isabelle d'Entremont

Herbes Salées

Laver les oignons ou échalottes et les tiges (jeunes préférés), poser en couches avec sel dans un grand pot de terre (cruche)
Le laisser reposer pour une semaine pour que ça développe du goût, avant de servir
Se garde pour une année et plus.

Ajouter cette assaisonnement Acadéenne aux soupes et aux ragoûts

Herbes Salées, pre-1945

CREAMY ONION SAUCE

Serves 4 to 6

1/4 cup (60 ml) butter
1 large onion, julienned
1 leek, cleaned, thinly sliced
1/4 cup (60 ml) flour
1/4 cup (60 ml) white wine
1 1/2 tsp (7 ml) grainy mustard
1 cup (250 ml) 35% cream
1 cup (250 ml) whole milk
1/2 lemon, juiced
fresh grated nutmeg
salt, pepper, to taste

Melt butter in medium-sized pot over medium heat, sweat onions and leeks until soft; do not brown. Add flour, cook 4 to 5 minutes until flour loses its raw flavour. Add wine, mustard, cream, and milk, cook stirring continuously until sauce begins to thicken. Continue cooking 4 minutes more while stirring. Add lemon, nutmeg, salt, and pepper.

Serve immediately over white fish of your choice. If sauce is made ahead, reheat slowly in double boiler.

"Sauce aux oignons is very good, a basic onion sauce that was used all the time to accompany everything. We enriched it to modern day— more butter, white wine, and grainy mustard for punch and colour. We added some leek and it brought out flavour. The lemon took it home."

ALAIN BOSSE, THE KILTED CHEF

Isabelle
d'Entremont

Sauce aux oignons

1/4 tasse de beurre   1 1/2 tasses d'eau
1/4 tasse de farine
1/4 cuillère à thé de sel
1/8 cuillère à thé de poivre

Bouillir les oignons dans une tasse d'eau
avec le beurre, le sel et le poivre.
Mêler la farine dans une 1/2 tasse d'eau froide
Quand les oignons sont cuits, ajouter
la farine pour épaissir

servir avec de la morue salée.

Sauce aux Oignons, pre-1945

Galettes au Sucre, pre-1945

Isabelle d'Entremont

Galettes au sucre
pour les fêtes de Noël

1 tasse de sucre blanc
1 tasse de beurre ou lard
2 ou 3 oeufs
½ cuillère à thé de bicarbonate de soude
1 cuillère à thé de crème de tatre
2 tasses de farine
Bien crèmer le beurre, ajouter le sucre,
   ensuite ajouter les oeufs
Tamiser la farine, le soude
   ajouter au premier mélange
Rouler la pâte un peu mince
   Décorer les galettes avec quelques raisins
Cuire à une chaleur .   vife.

SUGAR COOKIES WITH FRUITED BUTTERCREAM FILLING

Yields 24 cookies

For Cookies
1 cup (250 ml) butter
1 cup (250 ml) white sugar
3 eggs
2 cups (500 ml) all-purpose flour
1/2 tsp (2 ml) baking soda
1 tsp (5 ml) cream of tartar
2 tbsp (30 ml) maple sugar

For Buttercream
3/4 cup (175 ml) butter
1/4 cup (60 ml) shortening
5 cups (1.1 litre) icing sugar

For Rhubarb Filling
3 cups (750 ml) rhubarb, chopped
1 cup (250 ml) water
1 tbsp (15 ml) Sugar Moon Farm
   maple syrup

For Blueberry Filling
1 cup (250 ml) blueberries
1/3 cup (75 ml) Vandyke's blueberry juice

Preheat oven to 350°F (175°C). Cream together butter and sugar. Add eggs one at a time, beating just to incorporate. Combine flour, baking soda, and cream of tartar, add to wet ingredients. Wrap dough with saran wrap, refrigerate 30 minutes. Place dough on floured surface and roll to 1/4-inch (0.6-cm) thickness. Cut into desired shapes, place on parchment-lined baking sheet, sprinkle cookies with maple sugar. Bake 13 minutes. Cool slightly then transfer to wire rack.

For buttercream, place butter and shortening in bowl of stand mixer, mix on high until airy, scraping sides as you go. Incorporate icing sugar a cup at a time, beating well after each addition. Divide buttercream into 2 bowls.

For fillings, boil rhubarb, water, and maple syrup in medium pot, over medium heat until liquid reduces by three-quarters. Drain in fine mesh strainer over bowl. Cook blueberries and juice in medium pot, over medium heat, until liquid is completely reduced.

To one buttercream bowl, add rhubarb mixture, gently fold together. Add more icing sugar if needed. Fold in blueberry mixture to second bowl. Pipe buttercream onto one sugar cookie and top with another.

"Sugar cookie is a classic in everyone's culture in some form or other. We elevated it for a different feel. Layering it with buttercream and blueberry and rhubarb gave us tangy and sweet. It gave it a different appeal. The colour of the cream turned out really well—flecks of red and almost a light purplish."

ALAIN BOSSE, THE KILTED CHEF

MOLASSES COOKIES WITH ZESTY DATE FILLING

Yields 12 cookies

For Date Filling
14 oz (400g) pitted dates
2 cups (500 ml) water
1/2 lemon, zested and juiced

For Cookies
2/3 cup (160 ml) shortening
1/2 cup (125 ml) sugar
1/2 cup (125 ml) molasses
1 egg
1/2 tsp (2 ml) cinnamon
1/2 tsp (2 ml) ginger
2 tsp (10 ml) baking soda
1 tsp (5 ml) salt
2 1/2 cups (625 ml) flour

Put dates, water, and lemon in medium pot, cook over medium heat until water has disappeared and mixture has thickened. Set aside to cool.

Cream shortening and sugar together, beat in molasses, add egg. Combine dry ingredients, add to wet, mix well. Refrigerate dough 30 minutes.

To assemble cookies, place dough on floured surface, roll into large rectangle about 1/4-inch (0.6-cm) thick. Place filling in centre of rectangle in vertical direction squaring up filling as you go. Trim top section of dough and fold over filling, trim bottom half so that it covers first fold. Square up sides, place on parchment-lined baking sheet. Bake 11 minutes, remove from oven, square up sides again, bake 2 minutes more. Allow to cool before slicing.

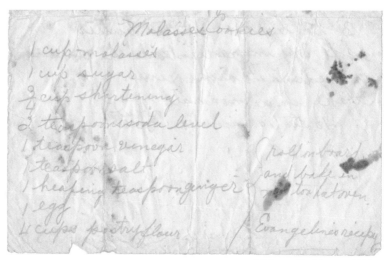

Molasses Cookies, pre-1945

"Molasses cookies back then would be a thicker cookie that held well in the cookie jar. We wanted to do something totally different like a Fig Newton—24 cookies, or 12 in the size we cut them. Nice, beautiful, firm cookie, nice texture of a date square or the idea of a square log. It turned out great."

ALAIN BOSSE, THE KILTED CHEF

WINTER SALAD

Serves 6

For Maple Balsamic Vinaigrette
1/2 cup (125 ml) canola oil
1/4 cup (60 ml) Acadian maple syrup
1/3 cup (75 ml) balsamic vinegar
1/2 tsp (2 ml) dry thyme
2 tsp (5 ml) Dijon mustard
1/2 tsp (2 ml) salt
1/4 tsp (1 ml) pepper

For Salad
8 oz (225 g) selected salad greens
1/2 cup (125 ml) red cabbage or kale,
  julienned
1/2 cup (125 ml) Brussels sprouts, shaved
1 cup (250 ml) cooked beets, peeled,
  cut into 1/2-inch (1 1/4-cm) dice
1/4 cup (60 ml) toasted walnuts
1/4 cup (60 ml) toasted pumpkin seeds
1/2 cup (125 ml) crumbled feta cheese

Combine vinaigrette ingredients in blender, mix until smooth. Toss salad greens, kale, and Brussels sprouts with vinaigrette. Top with beets, nuts, seeds, and sprinkle with feta.

WARTIME COOKBOOK — 1

Luncheons (

Winter Salad

For farm homes where fresh lettuce, etc., is not available in winter. Mix cold sliced potatoes and minced onion with your favorite salad dressing. Lay on bed of crisp inner leaves of cabbage. Make hollow in centre and empty into it a can of pears from which juice has been drained. Decorate with pickles, chow, or beets and hard boiled eggs. A few crisp sticks of raw turnips and carrots may be added—Mrs. Royal R. Simpson, Thomson Station, Nova Scotia.

* * * *

Winter Salad, 1945

"The original recipe was a good-looking kitchen cupboard salad, whatever you had kicking around your house in the dead of winter. First I thought we would use homemade sauerkraut, but we went with something more current and trendy with kale. The original salad is based on the idea you wouldn't have access to greens in the winter. We did a more modern take, keeping in mind the wintery goods we have on hand in Nova Scotia."

ALAN CROSBY, WHITE POINT BEACH RESORT

WARM ROASTED SWEET POTATO AND CHORIZO SALAD

Serves 8 as a side

3 lb (1.3 kg) sweet potatoes, peeled and
   diced in 1/2-inch (1 1/4-cm) cubes
2 tbsp (30 ml) olive oil
1 tsp (5 ml) salt
1/2 tsp (2 ml) pepper

For Chorizo
10 oz (300 g) ground Nova Scotia pork
2 tbsp (30 ml) olive oil
1 tsp (5 ml) smoked paprika
1/2 tsp (2 ml) salt
1/2 tsp (2 ml) pepper
2 tbsp (30 ml) ground cumin
1 tsp (5 ml) rubbed oregano
1/2 tsp (2 ml) garlic powder
1 tsp (5 ml) crushed chili flakes

For Dressing
3/4 cup (175 ml) mayonnaise
1 tbsp (15 ml) orange zest
2 tbsp (30 ml) orange juice
1 tbsp (15 ml) sugar
1 tsp (5 ml) smoked paprika
1/2 tsp (2 ml) pepper
1 tsp (5 ml) oregano
1/4 tsp (1 ml) cayenne pepper
1/2 tsp (2 ml) crushed chili flakes

3 tbsp (45 ml) chopped cilantro
4 green onions, chopped

To roast sweet potatoes, toss with oil, salt, and pepper. Roast on cookie sheet 20 minutes at 375°F (190°C) until tender and browned on edges.

For chorizo, add pork and oil to frying pan along with spices. Cook until just done, stirring frequently to break up clumps.

For dressing, combine all ingredients, stir to mix. Toss sweet potatoes with chorizo and dressing, stir gently to mix, add chopped cilantro and green onions, serve warm or at room temperature. Make in advance and re-warm, if desired. Makes delicious stand-alone salad or as side for grilled chicken or salmon.

"The original recipe is pretty basic; warm potatoes tossed with a simple vinaigrette. Many recipes from the '30s and '40s reflect a time when cooks' pantries were not as vast as what we enjoy today and many recipes reflected the austerity of the time. It certainly was present in my early life. My mother didn't waste anything. We went with something a lot more modern and used local products. It's a wonderful, edgy combo."

ALAN CROSBY, WHITE POINT BEACH RESORT

Hot Potato Salad

4 cups diced potatoes
4 strips breakfast bacon, diced
¼ cup chopped onion
¼ cup celery
¼ cup cider vinegar
¼ cup water
½ teaspoon white sugar
½ teaspoon salt
¼ teaspoon dry mustard
¼ teaspoon pepper

Scrub 6 potatoes and cook them in their jackets. While still warm, peel and dice them. Dice the bacon, pan fry till crisp. Add the chopped onions and celery. Cook and stir till tender. Add to the diced potatoes. Combine the vinegar, water, sugar, salt, pepper and mustard. Heat to boiling. Pour over the potato mixture. Blend well and serve hot.—Mrs. John Shearer, Hilden, Nova Scotia.

* * * *

Hot Potato Salad, 1945

UNIACKE ESTATE MUSEUM PARK

SEAFOOD CHOWDER

Serves 6

1 cup (250 ml) salt fish pieces

2 cups (500 ml) cold water

7 strips dry cured bacon, diced

1 cup (250 ml) onion, fine dice

1 rib celery, about 1/2 cup (125 ml)
   fine dice

1/2 tsp (2 ml) dry thyme

1 tbsp (15 ml) Montreal steak spice

4 cups (1 litre) diced potatoes such as
   Yukon Gold

2 cups (500 ml) 10% coffee cream

3 cups (750 ml) whole milk

2 tbsp (30 ml) potato starch

1/2 cup (125 ml) cold water

8–10 oz (225–300 g) raw salmon, diced

6–8 oz (170–225 g) hot smoked salmon
   belly such as St. Mary's River, diced

Rinse salt fish 3 times, soak in water 30 minutes.
In large pot add bacon, cook until almost crisp. Do
not drain fat. Add onions and celery, cook on low until
tender. Add thyme and steak spice.

Drain salt fish, reserving water in medium pot. Add
potato, bring to boil, cook until just barely tender. Dice
salt fish into small pieces, add to onion-bacon mix, cook
5 minutes on low. Add cream and milk, bring to bare
simmer. Stir together potato starch and water, whisk
into cream mix, simmer.

Add raw salmon and cooked potatoes along with boiling
water, gently simmer 5 minutes. Add hot smoked
salmon, season to taste.

A staple of Nova Scotia cuisine, seafood chowder
features the best of local seafood.

*"A practical everyday chowder that harkens
back to the roots of the original—and gluten free
to give a nod to our current culinary scene. One
big change—the original called for a 20-minute
boil to cook the fish! In this version all of the
fish is gently cooked in the barely simmering
chowder. The use of hot smoked salmon bellies
broadens the flavour and makes it a natural
pair with our Tidal Bay wines."*

ALAN CROSBY, WHITE POINT BEACH RESORT

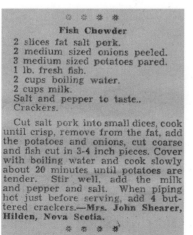

Fish Chowder, 1945

NOVA SCOTIA SMOKY LAMB STEW WITH CRANBERRIES

Serves 6

2 lb (900 g) lamb leg chops
1 onion, chopped
1/4 smoked lamb chop, or 4 strips smoked
  bacon, chopped
3 cloves garlic, chopped
3 tbsp (45 ml) all-purpose flour
9 cups (2.1 litres) beef or lamb stock
2 medium carrots, peeled and cut
12 green beans, trimmed and halved
4 tomatoes, peeled and crushed
1 cup (250 ml) fresh or frozen cranberries
salt, pepper, fresh or dried rosemary,
  to taste

Trim fat from chops, place in heavy stew pot. Cook to render fat. (If desired, use some fat and bones to make lamb stock.) Cut meat into bite-size cubes. Remove all but about 3 tbsp (45 ml) of fat from stew pot, add meat and brown. Reserve meat.

Cook onion in remaining fat with smoked meat. Add garlic, cook 2 minutes. Add flour, stirring until it starts to brown lightly. Stir in stock. Add reserved meat. Simmer over medium-low heat 45 minutes or until meat is tender.

Add carrots, cook 5 to 10 minutes. Add beans, tomatoes, and cranberries. Cook 5 minutes more. Season to taste.

"That recipe is a hoot. What's Syrian about it? There's no flavour development. Everything was dumbed down during the war. No one would make that stew today; you need stock and other vegetables. I'm trying to give people more full-bodied flavours you need today. It's more Nova Scotian now, with Nova Scotia lamb and cranberries. And there's a Syrian population now bringing in their own recipes."

HOWARD SELIG, VALLEY FLAXFLOUR

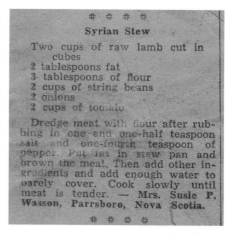

Syrian Stew, 1945

UNIACKE ESTATE MUSEUM PARK

✳ ✳ ✳ ✳

Oat Cakes

3 cups of fine oatmeal

1-2 cup flour (measuring cup)

1 spoonful soda

A pinch of salt

4 or 5 large tablespoons of molasses

1-2 cup shortening or lard

Method: Mix oatmeal, flour, soda and salt together, and then mix in shortening. When well mixed add molasses and mix well, and wet all with cold water. Avoid making it too soft. Roll out quite thin, cut in squares any size. — **Mrs. Fraser Langille, R.R. 2, River John, Nova Scotia.**

✳ ✳ ✳ ✳

Oat Cakes, 1945

DARK CHOCOLATE AND MAPLE CARAMEL OATCAKES WITH SEA SALT

Yields 8 large or 16 small oatcakes

1/4 cup (60 ml) + 1 tbsp (15 ml) coconut oil

1/4 cup (60 ml) + 1 tbsp (15 ml) butter

1/3 cup (75 ml) Acadian maple syrup

1/4 cup (60 ml) natural Greek yogurt

1 cup (250 ml) Speerville rolled oats

1/2 cup (125 ml) Speerville steel cut oats

1/2 cup (125 ml) all-purpose flour

1/2 cup (125 ml) Speerville Kamut flour

2 tbsp (30 ml) Valley Flaxflour golden flax flour

2 tbsp (30 ml) shredded unsweetened coconut (optional)

1/2 tsp (2 ml) baking soda

1 tsp (5 ml) salt

For Maple Caramel Sauce
1 cup (250 ml) white sugar

1/4 cup (60 ml) Acadian maple syrup

1 tbsp (15 ml) water

3 tbsp (45 ml) butter

2/3 cup (160 ml) cream

For Chocolate Drizzle
1/2 cup (125 ml) Just Us dark chocolate

coarse sea salt, for garnish

Cream together coconut oil, butter, maple syrup, and yogurt. In mixing bowl combine oats, flours, coconut, baking soda, and salt. Add liquid ingredients to dry ingredients, mix together by hand. Roll out between 2 sheets parchment paper to 10-inch (25-cm) square or 9-inch (23-cm) square for softer oatcakes. Cut into squares or triangles with pizza cutter and transfer to lined baking sheet. Bake at 350°F (175°C) 12 to 15 minutes.

Prepare caramel sauce by boiling sugar, maple syrup, and water 5 minutes. Then add butter and cream, stir well. In separate pot, melt chocolate.

Allow oatcakes to cool 5 minutes on pan before transferring to cooling rack. Drizzle with caramel and melted chocolate, sprinkle sea salt.

"I absolutely love oatcakes and I try them any chance I get. I grew up in Cape Breton and now live on the South Shore, and the oatcakes are radically different in each place. They are such a staple in Nova Scotia—the energy bars from 'back in the day.' The original is a simple recipe using what was available. This is exactly why your great-grandmother's recipe never turns out the way you remember; their spoonfuls and pinches are impossible to replicate. This recipe represents everything I love in an oatcake—a good crunch on the outside, loads of nutrients inside, and that salty-sweet flavour."

VANESSA MacDONALD, FIRESIDE KITCHEN

BIG SPRUCE KITCHEN PARTY PALE ALE SWISS STEAK

Serves 4

4 8-oz (225-g) round or flank steaks
1/3 cup (75 ml) flour
1 tbsp (15 ml) salt and pepper
1 tbsp (15 ml) smoked paprika
1 tbsp (15 ml) oregano
splash oil, for frying
2 tbsp (30 ml) chopped garlic
1 cup (250 ml) julienned red and green
   bell peppers
1 cup (250 ml) sliced mushroom
1 cup (250 ml) julienned red onion
1 cup (250 ml) halved cherry tomato
1 355-ml bottle (about 1 1/2 cups)
   Big Spruce Kitchen Party Pale Ale
2 cups (500 ml) beef stock
1 tbsp (15 ml) Worcestershire sauce
1 tbsp (15 ml) Tabasco
garlic baguette, grilled

Pound meat out with meat mallet on cutting board to tenderize. Dredge meat with flour and seasonings. Fry each side with hot oil in large pan. Remove steak, add garlic, peppers, mushroom, onion, and tomato. Deglaze pan with ale, then add beef stock, Worcestershire, and Tabasco.

Return steaks to pan, cover, simmer 2 hours.

Serve on wedge of grilled baguette accompanied by roasted baby potatoes.

"Swiss steak is not something I grew up with, but I like that original recipe. The recipe just called for water so the stock would not have been very flavourful, however. Big Spruce is a local beer. I switched it up with beer and beef stock and made it really 'stewy.'"

MIKE ELDERSHAW, MEMBERTOU CENTRE

Try This Over On Your Palate!

Swiss Steak
2 lbs. round steak 1″ thick
⅓ cup flour
1 tsp. salt
⅛ tsp. pepper
1 slice onion
2 cups boiling water or
1 cup water and 1 cup strained
   tomatoes.
Method:
1. Wipe meat; place on board.
2. Dredge with mixed flour and seasonings.
3. Pound flour into meat, using wooden potato mixer or edge of heavy plate.
4. Heat frying pan very hot; put in fat.
5. Brown meat on each side.
6. Add onion, boiling water and tomato. (Tomato soup may be used.)
7. Cover tightly. Cook below boiling point 2 hours.
Note: Nellie Lyle Pattinson (whose recipe this is) says that this may also be cooked in a Casserole in the oven and that green peppers may be added. **NOTE AGAIN:** *Two Hours?* Is she kidding? That's just about *thirty minutes* work for a pressure cooker.

Swiss Steak, 1948

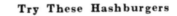

Try These Hashburgers

1-1 lb. can corned beef hash
5 soft round buns
Butter
¼ lb. sliced processed American
Cheddar cheese
Pickle relish

Preheat pan or broiler. Cut hash into five slices; broil until golden brown on one side; turn and brown the other side. Meanwhile split and butter buns. Place slice of cheese on either side of browned hash. Place buns on broiler rack. Broil until cheese is bubbly and buns are toasted. Remove from broiler. Top cheese with a little pickle relish. On each plate, place 2 bun halves, one topped with hash and cheese. Makes 5 servings.

Try These Hashburgers, 1948

TRY THESE SMOKED BEEF BRISKET SANDWICHES

Serves 5

2 lbs (900 g) smoked beef brisket
1 cup (250 ml) julienned onion
5 pretzel buns
1/4 cup (60 ml) butter
5 slices Oka cheese
1/4 cup (60 ml) mustard pickles
other pickles or sauerkraut, for garnish
  (optional)
handful fresh, crisp greens

Fry smoked meat and onions in heated medium frying pan.

Cut buns in half, spread butter, toast on grill. Pile meat on buns, top with cheese and mustard pickles.

Top with greens to serve. Pairs well with charred cabbage salad (page 156).

"I never tried corned beef hash. I was working in a café in Alberta and had to serve it, but couldn't bring myself to try it. But smoked beef brisket is delicious. Processed American cheddar cheese doesn't sound good at all so I replaced it with Oka."

MIKE ELDERSHAW, MEMBERTOU CENTRE

CHARRED CABBAGE SALAD WITH MAPLE MANGO DRESSING

Serves 5

1 medium cabbage
1/4 cup (60 ml) olive oil
salt, pepper, to taste
1 1/2 cups (375 ml) crispy fried
   parsnip chips
1 red apple, fine julienne
1 large carrot, fine julienne
1 cup (250 ml) mango purée
1/4 cup (60 ml) mayo
1/4 cup (60 ml) local maple syrup
1/2 cup (125 ml) local apple cider vinegar
1 beet, finely shaved
1 bunch scallions, finely sliced
5 lime wedges

Cut cabbage into 6 equal wedges, leaving core intact. Brush with olive oil, season with salt and pepper. Char both sides of cabbage wedges on broiler, barbecue, or open flame.

Shave 1 or 2 parsnips with vegetable peeler, deep-fry until golden brown and crispy. Set aside.

Place 5 cabbage wedges on individual plates. Shred remaining wedge in mixing bowl. Add apple and carrot, combine well.

Mix mango purée, mayo, syrup, and vinegar. Add to cabbage mixture, saving a bit to drizzle.

To serve, drizzle dressing on each cabbage wedge, top with cabbage mixture, garnish each with beets, parsnip, scallions, and lime wedges.

"I grew up in Alberta, but in an African Nova Scotia family. We'd come home to Dartmouth in the summer. Cabbage salad was often part of our meals. I'd done a grilled cabbage salad in a cooking contest, a burger competition, and it went over well, so I thought I'd try a spin off that. Charred cabbage gives it a depth of flavour, like a grilled Caesar salad."

MIKE ELDERSHAW, MEMBERTOU CENTRE

CABBAGE SALAD

Raw cabbage rates high as a vitamin-rich food, and it may be used in a large number of appetizing salads. The cabbage for salads should be crisp, and should be shredded as finely as possible. Remove and discard the coarse outer leaves and the core.

The shredded cabbage may be combined with celery, nuts, hard-cooked eggs, chopped apples, chopped onion, red and green sweet pepper, chopped carrots, cooked or canned peas and other vegetables. It combines well with flaked canned salmon. Use a good dressing to bind the salad together.

Cabbage Salad, 1949

Chapter 6

A LITTLE MORE MODERN

While the *What's Cooking?* online exhibition focuses on earlier years in the province's culinary history, it also includes recipes from the 1970s that remain classics of Nova Scotia cuisine. The writer of a 1973 letter to the editor of *GRASP*, a Black United Front publication published in Halifax, shares recipes from an American source for what she described as "soul food dishes," such as cornbread and sweet potato pie.

A 1975 issue of *Le Petit Courrier* newspaper, from Yarmouth, has a recipe for traditional Acadian rappie pie, or pâté a la rapure. And we are sharing several recipes from a Native Communications Society's collection that was distributed in a 1977 issue of *Micmac News*, a newspaper that was published in the province for twenty-six years. These include traditional bannock, corn casserole, and rabbit stew. While flavours, techniques, and food styles change, many popular recipes endure as part of Nova Scotia's food culture.

Facing page: An Acadian camp cook from Saulnierville Station bakes bread at mid-morning in 1950. (Alexander H. Leighton, Nova Scotia Archives, 198-413 negative 2952-d)

JALAPEÑO AND SMOKED GOUDA CORNBREAD

Yields 12 slices

1/4 cup (60 ml) fresh jalapeño
1 cup (250 ml) cornmeal
1 cup (250 ml) all-purpose flour
2 tbsp (30 ml) baking powder
1/2 cup (125 ml) milk
1/4 cup (60 ml) cream corn
1/4 cup (60 ml) grated smoked Gouda
2 tbsp (30 ml) melted butter

Char jalapeños on a barbecue, broiler, or open flame. Cool, seed, core, and rough chop.

Combine dry ingredients. Mix in milk, cream corn, jalapeños, Gouda, and butter, mix well.

Grease cast-iron pan, spread mixture evenly. Bake at 400°F (204°C) 30 to 35 minutes.

"Coming home to Nova Scotia in the summers, I grew up with a lot of barbecue, cornbread, and sweet potato pie. Cornbread was pretty traditional. Turns out the lady who wrote the recipe in 1973 lived two streets over from where I live right now in Sydney. We've had cornbread on a few menus over the years, so we played with it. I love jalapeño and smoked Gouda and it works well."

MIKE ELDERSHAW, MEMBERTOU CENTRE

CORN BREAD

¾ cup corn meal
¾ cup sifted all-purpose flour
3 teasp. baking powder
1 tablespoon sugar

¾ cup milk
2 tablespoons melted bacon drippings or vegetable oil

Grease an 8 x 8 x 2 inch baking pan. Combine all dry ingredients together in a bowl, add milk and oil, beat well, pour in pan. Bake in hot oven (425°) for 20 minutes or until lightly browned. Serve hot. Makes 6 servings.

Corn Bread, 1973

SWEET POTATO TART WITH
MAPLE-GLAZED PECAN AND BACON

Serves 4

1 1/2 cups (375 ml) sweet potato purée

1/2 cup (125 ml) butternut squash purée

1 tbsp (15 ml) cinnamon

1 tsp (5 ml) nutmeg

1 tsp (5 ml) cardamom

1 1/2 cups (375 ml) brown sugar

1 tbsp (15 ml) vanilla

3 large eggs

9-inch (23-cm) tart shell

1 cup (250 ml) crisp bacon bits

1 cup (250 ml) chopped pecans

1 cup (250 ml) local maple syrup

whipped cream, for topping

Preheat oven to 400°F (204°C). Combine all ingredients, except bacon, pecans, and maple syrup, in stand mixer, adding eggs last. Pour mixture into shell, bake 25 to 30 minutes or until filling is firm.

Toss bacon, pecans, and maple syrup in mixing bowl. Place on baking sheet, bake 7 to 8 minutes at 400°F (204°C). Top pies with warm crumble. Finish with fresh whipped cream.

Sweet potatoes and butternut squash are just two of many of Nova Scotia's wonderful locally grown vegetables, found throughout the province in farmers' markets and grocery stores.

SWEET POTATO PIE

9 in. unbaked pie shell	½ teas. allspice
1½ cups mashed, cooked or canned sweet potato	1½ cup sugar
1 teasp. ground cinnamon	1 teaspoon vanilla
½ teas. ground nutmeg	3 eggs slightly beaten

Combine sweet potato, milk, sugar, cinnamon, nutmeg, allspice and vanilla, stir until blended. Beat in eggs, turn in pastry shell. Bake in hot oven (450°) for 10 minutes, lower temperature to (350°) and bake 30 minutes, longer or until filling is firm.

Well I do hope you will try these recipes sometime and now bye-bye. Happy Eating.

Sweet Potato Pie, 1973

"I've eaten a lot of sweet potato pies. As a kid I just loved it. For this one, the bacon and pecan crumble adds a salty, sweet, and crunchy flavour. The profile is not just one note like a pumpkin pie. And the whipped cream finishes it off."

MIKE ELDERSHAW, MEMBERTOU CENTRE

Serves 6 to 8

4-lb (1.8-kg) chicken, cut into pieces
1 medium onion, diced

For filling
1 large onion, diced
4 large carrots, diced
3 stalks celery, diced
1/2 cup (125 ml) butter
1/2 cup (125 ml) flour
5 cups (1.1 litres) chicken stock
1 tbsp (15 ml) summer savory
salt, pepper, to taste
6 lbs (2.7 kg) potatoes, peeled

Place chicken in large soup pot, cover with water, add onions, boil until meat falls from bone. When cooked, separate meat and bones, set aside. Reserve stock.

For filling, place onion, carrot, and celery in medium pot, cover with water, boil until tender. Drain, set aside.

Melt butter in large pot, add flour, cook 4 to 5 minutes, stirring constantly until flour loses its raw flavour. Add stock and summer savory, cook until thick. Stir in vegetables and chicken, season with salt and pepper.

Grate potatoes with fine mesh grater. Place potatoes in cheesecloth and squeeze water into large bowl. Measure this water and add equal amount of cooking broth back into potatoes, mix well. Place half potato mixture in greased 9- x 13- inch (23- x 33-cm) pan. Top with filling, then remaining potatoes. Cook in preheated 400°F (204°C) oven 2 hours or until top is golden brown.

"The recipe that was given to us came out of a newspaper article; the ingredients were pretty basic. In fairness, rappie pie is pretty basic. We gave it a modern feel so it would appeal to more than Acadians. We grew up with it, usually served with molasses; it's gluttony and wet and is sometimes crispy on top. We made it like a layered rappie pie with a potato base."

ALAIN BOSSE, THE KILTED CHEF

Pâté à la Râpure

volaille de 5 ou 6 livres
⅔ seau de patates
2 oignons moyens, hachés finement
sel et poivre

fisamment grasse, faire fondre un morceaux de lard et ajoutez au mélange).

Mme Orey LeBlanc
Mavillette, N.-E.

Découpez par morceaux une volaille bien grasse. Couvrir avec de l'eau. Ajoutez les oignons, sel et poivre. Cuire— Plurez, lavez et râpez les patates (notant la quantité). Épurez dans un sac (2 tasses à la fois) jusqu'à ce que la préparation soit sèche. Placez dans un bol.
— Quand les patates sont complètement épurées, les défaire avec les mains dans un grand vaisseau. Ajoutez le bouillon chaud de la volaille, brassant bien. Si le bouillon ne donne pas la même quantité de mélange qu'avant d'avoir épurer les patates, ajoutez de l'eau bouillante. Sel et poivre au goût.
Grassez moule 17 x 12. Etendre la moitié du mélange. Distribuez la volaille. Couvrir de l'autre moitié de mélange.
Cuire à 400 dégrées pour deux heures pour obtenir une croûte bien dorée. (Note: Si la volaille n'est pas suf-

FEL
ORGAN

E. M. C

Pâté a la rapure, 1975

MAPLE POPCORN BALLS

Yields 10 quarts popcorn balls

1 1/2 cups (375 ml) Acadian maple syrup
1/2 cup (125 ml) unsalted butter
5 cups (1.1 litres) icing sugar
2 cups (500 ml) marshmallows
4 tbsp (60 ml) water
10 quarts (10 litres) popped popcorn

In large pot combine all ingredients except popcorn. Heat mixture to boil, then immediately reduce to simmer. Add popcorn, coat all evenly. Let cool enough to touch.

Then, wearing gloves, quickly shape into equal-sized balls. (Cooking spray prevents it from sticking to fingers.) Cool, place in airtight container until ready to eat.

"The popcorn balls were fun and tasty. I couldn't wait to try the popcorn out; it's great for kids for a snack. Molasses is very popular, I know. Older people relate to it—baked bread and molasses was always a treat— but we thought we'd try maple instead."

SHAUN ZWARUN, MEMBERTOU CENTRE

POPCORN BALLS

1 cup dark molasses
½ cup sugar
½ cup water
2 tablespoons cider vinegar
1 tablespoon butter
¼ teaspoon baking soda
3 quarts popped corn

1. Mix the molasses, sugar, water, vinegar and butter in a heavy saucepan. Bring to a boil, stirring just until sugar is dissolved.
2. Boil without stirring until mixture registers 290 degrees on a candy thermometer. Stir in baking soda.
3. Pour mixture over the corn and let it stand until cool. With the hands, shape into two inch balls.
Yield: three dozen

Popcorn Balls, 1977

LUSKINIGN

*Yields 1 batch traditional
native quick bread*

8 cups (1.8 L) flour
1/3 cup (75 ml) baking powder
1 1/4 cups (300 ml) sugar
2 tsp (10 ml) sea salt
2 cups (500 ml) shortening
4 cups (1 litre) milk
3 tbsp (45 ml) minced chives, optional

In large mixing bowl, combine all dry ingredients. Add shortening, mix until texture is crumbly.

Add milk and chives, mix until combined. Transfer onto baking sheet lined with parchment paper.

Dough will be one mass, not uniform in shape. Place into preheated 350°F (175°C) oven, bake 25 to 35 minutes or until done. Check it by inserting skewer into thickest part. Dough should stick to it.

Serve warm with butter and molasses.

"Bannock, or luski, is something that came very easily to me as it's a big part of the Native culture here. Modern bannock was introduced by the Scots, although Indigenous people had their own version before that. It has stayed pretty much the same. We make it every day for one reason or another—a meeting or a snack. You have to eat it that day as it doesn't hold up well. We hardly changed it at all; we added chives. A lot of the older people wonder why we play around with something that's already so good."

SHAUN ZWARUN, MEMBERTOU CENTRE

BANNOCK

2½ cups all purpose flour
5 teaspoons baking powder
½ teaspoon salt
2 tablespoons sugar
2 tablespoons lard
1 egg, optional
1 cup water

Combine flour, baking powder, salt and sugar in clean pail. Add lard. Rub to form fine crumbs. If using egg, combine with water. Add to flour mixture. Stir to form soft dough. Knead until smooth, about 10 seconds.

Lightly grease heavy cast iron skillet with lard. Dust with flour. Place ½ dough in pan. Heat pan over live coals for five (5) minutes. Raise pan to 1½ feet above coals. Bake five to ten minutes longer or until underside is lightly brown and crusty. Turn and bake on the other side about 10-12 minutes. Bake remaining dough as above. Yield: Two bannocks or about six to eight servings.

Taken from: ::A Genuine First Wilderness Kingdom, New Cook Book"

Bannock, 1977

INDIAN CORN SCALLOP
2 cups corn
2 cups milk
1 teaspoon salt
1 teaspoon sugar
Thicken with 2 tablespoons flour and 2
eggs and add 2 tablespoons of butter.
Mix in order given and cook slowly 30
minutes.

Indian Corn Scallop, 1977

DRAGON'S BREATH BLUE CHEESE CORN BAKE

Serves 4 to 6

3 cups (750 ml) fresh corn niblets
1/2 cup (125 ml) diced vidalia onion
1/2 cup (125 ml) diced celery
1/2 cup (125 ml) diced red pepper
1/2 cup (125 ml) diced green pepper
1 cup (250 ml) cream
1/4 cup (60 ml) panko
2 eggs
2 tbsp (30 ml) honey
2 tbsp (30 ml) crushed pink peppercorns
sea salt, to taste
1/2 cup (125 ml) Dragon's Breath
  blue cheese
3 tbsp (45 ml) minced chives

Preheat oven to 350°F (175°C). Spray medium casserole dish with cooking spray or rub with butter.

In large mixing bowl, combine all ingredients except blue cheese and chives. Check seasonings. Pour ingredients into casserole dish, place in oven 30 to 40 minutes.

Add crumbled cheese, bake 3 to 4 minutes until cheese is heated. Garnish with chives or other fresh herbs.

"In Native culture, squash, corn, and beans are three sisters. We do a lot with corn at the Centre. It's a staple. As a chef I love corn. Basically it looked like a cream-corn dish so we did a corn gratin with panko and blue cheese. We tried to do something a little more modern and use as many local products as possible such as Dragon's Breath blue cheese."

SHAUN ZWARUN, MEMBERTOU CENTRE

HEARTY RABBIT STEW

Serves 4 to 6

2 rabbits, cut into pieces
sea salt, to taste
2 tbsp (30 ml) unsalted butter
2 cups (500 ml) pearl onion
1 tsp (5 ml) minced garlic
1 cup (250 ml) diced leek
1 cup (250 ml) medium diced celery
2–3 sprigs fresh thyme
2 tbsp (30 ml) pink peppercorns
3 bay leaves
2 tbsp (30 ml) all-purpose flour
1/4 cup (60 ml) Phone Box Red or a
   medium bodied red wine
4 cups (1 litre) stock, preferably game
   (or beef or chicken)
1 cup (250 ml) diced parsnip
2 cups (500 ml) diced carrot
1 cup (250 ml) diced turnip
1 cup (250 ml) sour cream
2 tbsp (30 ml) each, cornstarch and
   water, if necessary

Season rabbit pieces with sea salt, set aside for 15 minutes.

In preheated heavy-bottom pot, brown rabbit on all sides with 1 tbsp butter. Remove from pot, add remaining butter, onions, garlic, leek, celery, and herbs. Sauté 2 to 3 minutes, then add flour. Stir often until flour starts to turn brown—4 to 5 minutes. Add wine to deglaze. After 2 minutes return rabbit to pot, add stock, and cover.

After about 1 hour, add remaining vegetables. Continue to simmer until rabbit is done and vegetables are tender, 30 to 45 minutes. Add sour cream, adjust seasoning if desired.

If too thin, thicken with cornstarch slurry.

WILD RABBIT

Skin and clean very good and soak in salt water a few mintutes. It can be roasted like the wold duck, or baked in oven with broad dressing, made with two cups of crumbled corn bread, moistened with a little water. Add three tablespoons onion, chopped or minced, and salt and pepper and a little sage (optional). Pack inside the rabbit, and baste with drippings or fat while roasting. Young rabbits can also be salted andpeppered and rolled in flour and fried in hot grease, as you would a young chicken. Older rabbits can be stewed and corn dumplings added.

Wild Rabbit, 1977

"I was inspired by several of the rabbit recipes in the old newspaper. We've done rabbit here in this First Nations community. A lot is passed down from generation to generation. This stew hasn't changed a whole lot in a hundred years. I was trying to make it more modern by adding more current and local ingredients, but not change the format."

SHAUN ZWARUN, MEMBERTOU CENTRE

Chef Biographies

Alexandra Beaulieu, Bulwark Cider Maker, Muwin Estate Wines, New Ross
Originally from Trois-Riviere, Quebec, Alexandra completed oenology training in France and worked in the wine industry in British Columbia and Quebec. A desire to live by the ocean brought her to Nova Scotia in 2015. The quality of life and the extraordinary people she met made her fall in love with the province. In 2016, the apple lover traded grapes for apples to become Bulwark's cider maker.

Chris Bolt, Chef, The Press Gang Restaurant & Oyster Bar, Halifax
With a Parisian background, Chris began cooking young. He studied culinary arts at the Culinary Institute of Canada (CIC), Charlottetown, Prince Edward Island, and travelled to Turkey with a knowledge exchange program for young cooks. Chris worked as: sous chef, Café Chianti; first cook, The Bicycle Thief; sous chef, restaurant chef, Agricola St. Brasserie; chef, Lion and Bright; consultant, The Reluctant Chef, St. John's, Newfoundland. He is passionate about local, seasonal, sustainably produced ingredients.

Alain Bosse, The Kilted Chef, Pictou
Alain is founder of Alain Bosse Consulting Ltd, bestselling author, *Saltscapes* magazine food editor, and Taste of Nova Scotia past president. In 2011 he was named the province's first Culinary Ambassador. Alain has represented Atlantic Canada at numerous trade shows and has been guest instructor at Louisiana's John Folse Culinary Institute and Cordon Bleu schools, among others. He is passionate about buying and eating local, and enjoys teaching children good food habits.

Jenner Cormier, Mixologist, Ironworks Distillery, Lunenburg
Jenner has ten years experience in the hospitality industry, training and working in bars in Halifax, Toronto, Europe, and the United States. He was named Canada's best bartender by winning *Diageo World Class Canada 2013* and *Canada's BOL's Around the World* competition. Jenner studied on scholarship in New York, and worked with the world's largest cocktail conventions. The Halifax native is a beverage professional who values great hospitality and memorable experiences.

Alan Crosby, Chef, White Point Beach Resort, White Point
Born and raised in Liverpool, Nova Scotia, Alan returned home in 2003 to become chef at White Point. After graduating from Mount Allison University, Sackville, New Brunswick, Alan attended the CIC in Charlottetown, Prince Edward Island. He spent fourteen years travelling the country with stops in Stratford, Ontario, working at the Church Restaurant; Charlottetown; Hotel Vancouver; and Deltas of Halifax. The perfect job was waiting by the sea.

Ingrid Dunsworth, The Cake Lady, Hubbards
Ingrid moved to the province in 1998 from Bavaria and happily switched careers from dental hygiene to cake making. She's a popular presence at farmers' markets in Halifax and Dartmouth, and on the Halifax waterfront, specializing in delicious German sweets. A highlight of Ingrid's life was an invitation to the private Highgrove Royal Gardens, the home of HRH Prince Charles and wife Camilla, who had enjoyed Ingrid's cakes.

Mike Eldershaw, Restaurant Chef, Membertou Trade and Convention Centre and Kiju's Restaurant, Membertou
Mike was born in Alberta with Nova Scotia roots and is a chef with over ten years experience at restaurants in Alberta, Saskatchewan, and Nova Scotia. Mike has plied his skills at the Membertou Centre for three years, two as restaurant chef. He has been enthusiastically working with the entire culinary team to build the reputation of Kiju's Restaurant.

Mark Gray, Executive Chef, Battery Park, Brooklyn Warehouse, ACE Burger Co., Halifax
Halifax native Mark started in the culinary industry at sixteen, washing dishes at Il Mercato. He worked in restaurants in Alberta, returning to Halifax where, at twenty, he became Co-Executive Chef at The Hilton Garden Inn, then the award-winning Brooklyn Warehouse. Mark earned his Canadian Red Seal Certification, completed culinary arts at Nova Scotia Community College (NSCC), and won gold in the prestigious Gold Medal Plates 2016 regional competition.

Jonathan Joseph, Chef/Owner, Ye Olde Argyler Lodge, Lower Argyle
Born and raised in Miami, Florida, Jonathan has worked in kitchens since he was fourteen. He graduated magna cum laude with degrees in hotel and restaurant management from Florida International University's Hospitality program. Jonathan has helped organize South Beach Food and Wine, one of the world's largest food and wine festivals. He made southwest Nova Scotia his home in 2007, bringing along his love and passion for food and hospitality.

Ben Kelly, Resident Chef, Kitchen Door Catering, Bedford

Ben was raised in and around Malagash, Nova Scotia, on a small hobby farm where the family grew vegetables and raised chickens and turkeys. With his mother and sisters, Ben foraged in the woods for berries and mushrooms. He knew when young he wanted to be a chef and worked in his first kitchen at fifteen. He has worked mainly in Nova Scotia, but also in Ontario, Quebec, and the Yukon.

Vanessa MacDonald, Bakery Supervisor, Fireside Kitchen, Prescott Group, Halifax

Vanessa hails from Mabou on Cape Breton Island. She studied confectionary arts at Bonnie Gordon School of Confectionary Arts in Toronto, and boulanger and baking art at NSCC. She loves sourcing and experimenting with the wealth of regional ingredients in Atlantic Canada. Vanessa finds that baking allows her to play into her strengths, allowing endless opportunities for creativity. She focuses on healthy and nutritional grains and loves to forage for chanterelle mushrooms.

Lynne MacKay, Co-owner, Ironworks Distillery, Lunenburg

In 2005 Lynne MacKay and Pierre Guevremont decided they wanted a change. They left behind their former lives in Ontario, returned to Nova Scotia, and four years later founded Ironworks Distillery in a heritage blacksmith shop in old town Lunenburg. The original mandate was to create fine spirits and liqueurs using only excellent local fruit, but the product line quickly expanded to include rum, made from Crosby's Fancy Molasses.

Beverly McClare, Creator, Tangled Garden, Grand Pré

Beverly is an artist, cook, and entrepreneur who started Tangled Garden in 1991. The Hillsvale, Hants County, native operated a small café in Wolfville before buying a house and acre of land, just waiting for her magic. She made and sold wreaths and dried flower bouquets, but she was soon inspired to create herb-infused products, starting with vinegars and then adding jellies, jams, chutneys, mustards, and liqueurs.

Aimee McDougall, Sous Chef, Governors Pub & Eatery, Sydney

Aimee started cooking at a young age helping with a family business, and continuing on to study culinary arts at NSCC, Marconi campus. Aimee and her team have won bronze medals in cooking competitions. She has also trained at the International Culinary Centre in New York. Aimee is passionate about food and is eager to learn, always up for new challenges or opportunities.

Tammy McKearney, Pastry Chef/Restaurant Manager, Lane's Privateer Inn, Liverpool
Originally from Dartmouth, Tammy worked in service positions for fifteen years in
Mahone Bay and Lunenburg at Mimi's Ocean Grill, Fleur de Sel, Trattoria Della Nonna, and
Lunenburg Arms. Five years ago she joined Lane's Privateer Inn. Inspired by the talented
chefs she has worked with in the industry, Tammy offers an authentic take on vegan,
"flexitarian," and gluten-free dishes, made with fresh, local ingredients.

Ardon Mofford, Executive Chef, Governors Pub & Eatery, Commoner Table & Tap, Sydney
From Montreal, Ardon grew up in St. Peter's, Cape Breton, where, at eleven, he assisted his
father at MacDonald's Hotel and Dining Room. He graduated in tourism marketing at Cape
Breton University and received Red Seal certification through NSCC. Committed to local
food, he has worked with *Right Some Good Food Festival* and was twice Gold Medal Plates
Bronze Medallist. Ardon's Celtic-Caribbean roots inspire his cuisine.

Wayne Odo, Pastry Chef, Governors Pub & Eatery, Sydney
Born and raised in Cape Breton, Wayne loved to bake in high school. At college he graduated
in electrical engineering. Years later he followed his passion and graduated in culinary arts
at NSCC Marconi. He began at Governors as a prep cook, working his way to pastry chef,
responsible for desserts and breads. He is part of a team that caters everything from small
group meals to hors d'oeuvres for 2000.

Stephanie Ogilvie, Head Chef, Brooklyn Warehouse, Halifax
With her grandmother's inspiration, Stephanie has been working in the culinary industry
since she was sixteen. The Moncton native attended the CIC in Charlottetown, Prince
Edward Island, followed by work in prestigious Toronto restaurants—George Restaurant,
Ultra Supper Club, and Canoe. Stephanie traveled to Australia, and eventually to Halifax
where she was sous chef and executive catering chef at Jane's on the Common before moving
on to Brooklyn Warehouse.

Henry Pedro, Brewer, Boxing Rock Brewing Company, Shelburne
Henry, a chemical engineer trained at Humber College and the University of Toronto, moved
to Shelburne in 2012. He started Boxing Rock along with another engineer with a passion
for beer, Emily Tipton. It might be a long way from his life as professional engineer and
manager at automotive, manufacturing, and other mechanical companies, but the successful
competitive sailor feels right at home on the Atlantic.

T. J. Pittman IV, Sous Chef, Old Fish Factory Restaurant, Lunenburg
Born and raised in Lunenburg, T. J. started in the restaurant industry while a student at Saint Mary's University in Halifax. Upon graduating, he went to Niagara College's Canadian Food and Wine Institute. After working for two years in that region, he returned home to work at Fleur de Sel, followed by two years work in Birmingham, England, including at a one-star Michelin restaurant. In 2015, Lunenburg beckoned again.

Andrew Prince, Executive Chef, Ace Burger Co., Halifax
Andrew began his culinary career in 2011, after graduating from the CIC in Charlottetown, Prince Edward Island. During his time at CIC, he began apprenticing under Halifax's best chefs, a journey that took him to Brooklyn Warehouse, Fid Resto, and Chives. In 2013, Andrew decided it was time to focus on the food he craves—late-night comfort food. He strives to continue bringing Halifax amazing burgers and expanding the vision of Ace.

Jonathan Rhyno, Chef, Lane's Privateer Inn, Liverpool
Born and raised in Liverpool, Jonathan grew up yearning to cook, so after graduating from high school he enrolled in culinary arts at NSCC Lunenburg campus. He has been cooking on the south shore for most of his life. The highlight of the dining experiences that Jonathan provides is embracing the fresh local ingredients found in the shops and on the farms in the Liverpool area.

Howard Selig, Chef/Co-owner, Valley Flaxflour Ltd., Middleton
Howard received his Inter-provincial Red Seal as Journeyman Cook in 1984. He volunteers with community initiatives and Canadian Association of Foodservice Professionals. Howard graduated from Acadia University in 1995 with honours in nutrition, soon becoming a registered dietitian. He and wife, Wendy Rodda, established Valley Flaxflour in 1998. Howard was inducted into the Canadian Culinary Federation Honour Society in 2014, recognized for his passion and service to the culinary profession.

Chris Velden, Chef/Co-owner, Flying Apron Inn & Cookery, Summerville
Chris hails from Frankfurt, Germany, and has cooked and taught across Canada, the US, and Europe, for over 40 years. Certified European master chef and culinary instructor's qualifications match his passion for teaching future chefs and the public. Through partnerships with many local farmers and producers, Chris supports sustainable and ethical farming. He is a member of Slow Food NS and a representative for Ocean Wise.

Shaun Zwarun, Executive Chef, Membertou Trade and Convention Centre and Kiju's Restaurant, Membertou

A Cape Breton native, Shaun's experience ranges over twenty-four years from small restaurants to grand hotels. His passion for food started young, working in the family garden and tending to ducks, chickens, and pigs, inspiring the farm-to-table approach he practises with his locally driven seasonal menus. Shaun networks with local suppliers creating innovative dishes to establish Kiju's as a leading culinary destination.

Detailed Citations for Archival Recipes

CHAPTER 1

IRISH POTATOE PUDING, 1786, Commissioner of Public Record, Nova Scotia Archives RG 1 vol. 411 no. 10

RICE PUDDING, 1800s, Almon Scrapbook, Nova Scotia Archives, MG 1 Vol 14 page 120

CHICKEN POT PIE, 1800s, Recipes Kept by Margaret Irons, Miscellaneous Manuscripts Nova Scotia Archives MG 100 vol. 213 no.6

LOBSTER PIE, 1809, MacGregor Miller Collection, Nova Scotia Archives, MG 1 vol. 652 no. 7 page 37

LEMON PICKLE, 1809, Miller Family Nova Scotia Archives MG 1 vol. 652 no. 7 page 23

MOLASSES GINGERBREAD, 1816-1886, Miller Family Collection, Nova Scotia Archives MG 1 vol. 693 folder 3

APPLE CAKE, circa 1830, Nova Scotia Military Nova Scotia Archives RG 22 vol. 13

CURRANT WINE, 1849, Nova Scotia Museum Uniacke Family Collection

ONE, TWO, THREE, FOUR CAKE, 1869, McQueen, Lowden Family Collection, Nova Scotia Archives MG 1 vol. 3349 no. 23

MRS. WILSON'S PUMPKIN PIES, 1874, Nova Scotia Museum Uniacke Family

CHICKEN SOUP FOR INVALIDS, 1874, Ben Church Hicks Collection, Nova Scotia Archives MG 1 vol. 2094 no. 9

DELICIOUS CUCUMBER PRESERVES, 1874, Ben Church Hicks Collection, MG 1 vol.2094 no. 9, Nova Scotia Archives

CHEESE TOAST, 1877, Almon Family Collection, Nova Scotia Archives MG 1 vol. 17 no. 43

FOR LUNCHEON, 1881, Miller Family Collection, Nova Scotia Archives MG 1 vol. 693 folder 3

GINGER BEER, 1882, Miller Family Collection Nova Scotia Archives MG 1 vol. 693 folder 3

CHAPTER 2

GRAVY SOUP, Mrs. William (Mary) Lawson and Miss Alice Jones, *Church of England Institute Receipt Book*, 1888, page 9, Nova Scotia Museum

OX TAIL SOUP, Mrs. William (Mary) Lawson and Miss Alice Jones, *Church of England Institute Receipt Book*, 1888, page 21, Nova Scotia Museum

HOW TO COOK A SALT CODFISH, Mrs. William (Mary) Lawson and Miss Alice Jones, *Church of England Institute Receipt Book*, 1888, page 21, Nova Scotia Museum

LOBSTER RISOTTO, Mrs. William (Mary) Lawson and Miss Alice Jones, *Church of England Institute Receipt Book*, 1888, page 31, Nova Scotia Museum

CROQUETTES OF CHICKEN, Mrs. William (Mary) Lawson and Miss Alice Jones, *Church of England Institute Receipt Book*, 1888, page 51, Nova Scotia Museum

RHUBARB MARMALADE, Mrs. William (Mary) Lawson and Miss Alice Jones, *Church of England Institute Receipt Book*, 1888, page 91, Nova Scotia Museum

PLUMS PRESERVED IN BRANDY, Mrs. William (Mary) Lawson and Miss Alice Jones, *Church of England Institute Receipt Book*, 1888, page 94, Nova Scotia Museum

COCKTAIL, Mrs. William (Mary) Lawson and Miss Alice Jones, *Church of England Institute Receipt Book*, 1888, page 101, Nova Scotia Museum

CHAPTER 3

STEWED OYSTERS, E. Lockett, *Cape Breton hand-book and tourist's guide*, 1890, page 123, Nova Scotia Archives V/F vol. 313 no. 27

CAULIFLOWER WITH WHITE SAUCE AND CHEESE, Helen N. Bell, *Elementary Text-Book of Cookery*, 1898, page 47, Nova Scotia Archives LT C77 B4

SAVORY POTATOES, Helen N. Bell, *Elementary Text-Book of Cookery*, 1898, page 49, Nova Scotia Archives LT C77 B4

FISH CAKES, BALLS, or RISSOLES, Helen N. Bell, *Elementary Text-Book of Cookery*, 1898, page 34, Nova Scotia Archives LT C77 B4

STEAK STEWED WITH VEGETABLES, Helen N. Bell, *Elementary Text-Book of Cookery*, 1898, page 36, Nova Scotia Archives LT C77 B4

SHEPHERD'S PIE, Helen N. Bell, *Elementary Text-Book of Cookery*, 1898, page 42, Nova Scotia Archives LT C77 B4

APPLE WATER, Helen N. Bell, *Elementary Text-Book of Cookery*, 1898, page 91, Nova Scotia Archives LT C77 B4

GENUINE BOSTON BAKED BEANS, Hattie & Mylius, Limited, Wholesale Druggist, *The Art of Cooking Made Easy*, 1900, page 31, Nova Scotia Museum 641.59716 H36 c.1

CURRIED LOBSTERS, 1900s, Robert Simpson & Co Collection, Nova Scotia Archives MG 6 vol. 31 no. 16, page 23

LEMON PIE, S.J. Sims and B.E. Hillspage, *Tried and True: A handbook of choice cooking recipes*, 1902, pages 17 and 18, Nova Scotia Archives TX 715 S61

ASPARAGUS CHEESE 1902, Nova Scotia Museum Uniacke Family Collection

STEAMED BROWN BREAD, The Ladies of All Saints Church Guild, *The Bedford Recipe Book*, 1910, page 18, Nova Scotia Museum 84.92.11

PEANUT SOUP, The Ladies of All Saints Church Guild, *The Bedford Recipe Book*, 1910, page 9, Nova Scotia Museum 84.92.11

GAELIC FRUIT CAKE, The Managers' Auxiliary of St. John's Church, Bridgewater, N.S., *The LaHave Cook Book* 1912, page 66, Nova Scotia Museum 641.59716 B85

SCALLOP CHOWDER, The Managers' Auxiliary of St. John's Church, Bridgewater, N.S., *The LaHave Cook Book* 1912, page 13, Nova Scotia Museum 641.59716 B85

CHAPTER 4
STRAWBERRY CUSTARD, various women's organizations, *The modern cook book for Nova Scotia and PEI*, circa 1920, page 144, Nova Scotia Archives TX 715 M689

STRAWBERRY SHORTCAKE, various women's organizations, *The modern cook book for Nova Scotia and PEI*, 1920, page 129, Nova Scotia Archives TX 715 M689

POP DOODLE, various women's organizations, *The modern cook book for Nova Scotia and PEI*, 1920, page 65, Nova Scotia Archives TX 715 M689

SALMON CROQUETTES 1921, Prat-Starr Family Collection, Nova Scotia Archives MG 1 vol. 2627 no. 17

MARMALADE 1921, Prat-Starr Family Collection, Nova Scotia Archives MG 1 vol. 2627 no. 17

CREOLE NEW POTATOES 1922, Prat-Starr Family Collection, Nova Scotia Archives MG 1 vol. 2627 no. 17

WINDSOR SANDWICHES 1922, Prat-Starr Family Collection, Nova Scotia Archives MG 1 vol. 2627 no. 17

MABLE GILSON'S CHOCOLATE CAKE 1922, Prat-Starr Family Collection, Nova Scotia Archives MG 1 vol. 2627 no. 17

PLANKED SHAD WITH POTATO 1922, Prat-Starr Family Collection, Nova Scotia Archives MG 1 vol. 2627 no. 17

SCALLOPED CLAMS 1922, Prat-Starr Family Collection, Nova Scotia Archives MG 1 vol. 2627 no. 17

MRS. FRAMPTONS TOMATO SOUP (M.R.S.) 1922, Prat-Starr Family Collection, Nova Scotia Archives MG 1 vol. 2627 no. 17

MULLIGATAWNY SOUP 1922, Prat-Starr Family Collection, Nova Scotia Archives MG 1 vol. 2627 no. 17

MEXICAN RABBIT 1922, Prat-Starr Family Collection, Nova Scotia Archives MG 1 vol. 2627 no. 17

CUMBERLAND DRESSING, Kent Vinegars, Canning, N.S., *Kent Vinegars Recipe Book and Household Hints*, circa 1930s, page 5, Nova Scotia Museum 88.74.15

COUNTRY CLUB EGGS, Farmers' Limited, Halifax, *Farmers' Milk Facts for Halifax*, circa 1936, page 8, Nova Scotia Museum 84.92.14

MAYFLOWER MEAT LOAF, Farmers' Limited, Halifax, *Farmer' Milk Facts for Halifax,* circa 1936, page 7, Nova Scotia Museum 84.92.14

CHAPTER 5
BLUEBERRY MUFFINS, Ladies' Aid of the Grand Pre United Church, *Grand-Pre Cook Book*, 1939, page7, Nova Scotia Museum 641.59716 G75

ANGELS ON HORSEBACK, Atlantic War Fund Club Halifax, *Favourite Recipes*, 1940, page 27, Nova Scotia Archives V/F vol. 541 no. 22

MAPLE PARFAIT, Atlantic War Fund Club Halifax, *Favourite Recipes*, 1940, page 20, Nova Scotia Archives V/F vol. 541 no. 22

GINGER SNAPS, Atlantic War Fund Club Halifax, *Favourite Recipes*, 1940, page 35, Nova Scotia Archives V/F vol. 541 no. 22

THREE-IN-ONE ROLLS, Sydney Nutrition Committee, *KITCHEN ARMY NUTRITION and RECEIPT BOOK*, circa 1943, page 24, Nova Scotia Archives V/F vol. 314 no. 2

BEAFSTEAK AND KIDNEY PIE, Sydney Nutrition Committee, *KITCHEN ARMY NUTRITION and RECEIPT BOOK*, circa 1943, page 28, Nova Scotia Archives V/F vol. 314 no. 2

BLUEBERRY BUCKLE, Sydney Nutrition Committee, *KITCHEN ARMY NUTRITION and RECEIPT BOOK*, circa 1943, page 18, Nova Scotia Archives V/F vol. 314 no. 2

WHOLE WHEAT CRANBERRY LOAF, Sydney Nutrition Committee, *KITCHEN ARMY NUTRITION and RECEIPT BOOK*, circa 1943, page 33, Nova Scotia Archives V/F vol. 314 no. 2

RAW CRANBERRY SALAD, Sydney Nutrition Committee, *KITCHEN ARMY NUTRITION and RECEIPT BOOK*, circa 1943, page 19, Nova Scotia Archives V/F vol. 314 no. 2

SOUPE AUX POISSON PRE-1945, Isabelle d'Entremont Collection, Musée des Acadiens des Pubnicos

HERBES SALÉES PRE-1945, Isabelle d'Entremont Collection, Musée des Acadiens des Pubnicos

SAUCE AUX OIGNONS PRE-1945, Isabelle d'Entremont Collection, Musée des Acadiens des Pubnicos

GALETTES AU SUCRE POUR LES FÊTES DE NOËL PRE-1945, Isabelle d'Entremont Collection, Musée des Acadiens des Pubnicos

MOLASSES COOKIES, pre-1945, Isabelle d'Entremont or Emiline Amirault Collection, Musée des Acadiens des Pubnicos

WINTER SALAD, *Halifax Herald and the Halifax Mail, WARTIME ECONOMY BOOK OF RECIPES FOR 1945*, April 10, 1945, page 12, Nova Scotia Archives MG 100 vol. 126 no. 12

HOT POTATO SALAD, *Halifax Herald and the Halifax Mail, WARTIME ECONOMY BOOK OF RECIPES FOR 1945*, April 10, 1945, page 12, Nova Scotia Archives MG 100 vol. 126 no. 12

FISH CHOWDER, *Halifax Herald and the Halifax Mail, WARTIME ECONOMY BOOK OF RECIPES FOR 1945*, April 10, 1945, page 6, Nova Scotia Archives MG 100 vol. 126 no. 12

SYRIAN STEW, 1945 *Halifax Herald and the Halifax Mail, WARTIME ECONOMY BOOK OF RECIPES FOR 1945*, April 10, 1945, page 18, Nova Scotia Archives MG 100 vol. 126 no. 12

OAT CAKES, 1945 *Halifax Herald and the Halifax Mail, WARTIME ECONOMY BOOK OF RECIPES FOR 1945,* April 10, 1945, page 24, Nova Scotia Archives MG 100 vol. 126 no. 12

SWISS STEAK, Carrie Best, *The Clarion—for Church and Community*, September 22, 1948, page 4, Nova Scotia Archives Microfilm 4340

TRY THESE HASHBURGERS, Carrie Best, *The Clarion—for Church and Community*, September 22, 1948, page 6, Nova Scotia Archives Microfilm 4340

CABBAGE SALAD, Carrie Best, *The Clarion—for Church and Community*, March 23, 1949, page 5, Nova Scotia Archives Microfilm 4340

CHAPTER 6

CORN BREAD, Dorothy Sparling, LETTERS TO THE EDITOR *GRASP*, February 1973, page 4, Nova Scotia Archives Grasp February 1973; microfilm 3785

SWEET POTATO PIE, Dorothy Sparling, LETTERS TO THE EDITOR *GRASP*, February 1973, page 4, Nova Scotia Archives Grasp February 1973; microfilm 3785

PATÉ A LA RÂPURE, Mme Orey LeBlanc, *Le Petit Courrier de la Nouvelle-Écosse*, July 10, 1975, Vol. 39, #10

POPCORN BALLS, Native Communications Society of Nova Scotia, *An Indian Cookbook*, 1977, page 3, *The Micmac News*, February 1977 Nova Scotia Archives V/F vol. 143 no. 2

BANNOCK, Native Communications Society of Nova Scotia, *An Indian Cookbook*, 1977, page 3, *The Micmac News*, February 1977 Nova Scotia Archives V/F vol. 143 no. 2

INDIAN CORN SCALLOP, Native Communications Society of Nova Scotia, *An Indian Cookbook*, 1977, page 3, *The Micmac News*, February 1977 Nova Scotia Archives V/F vol. 143 no. 2

WILD RABBIT, Native Communications Society of Nova Scotia, *An Indian Cookbook*, 1977, page 3, *The Micmac News*, February 1977 Nova Scotia Archives V/F vol. 143 no. 2

Acknowledgments

Thanks to staff from Nova Scotia Archives; Communities, Culture and Heritage; Communications Nova Scotia; Nova Scotia Museum; and Taste of Nova Scotia.

Select Nova Scotia, a provincial program created to encourage Nova Scotians to buy local, provided funding for this project. In addition, funding was received from the Canada 150 Fund.

Thanks to the fabulous chefs and industry professionals who offered their time, skills, and imagination to this book. Their recipes reflect the amazing variety, quality, and originality of Nova Scotia cuisine.

Thanks to Nimbus Publishing for taking on the project.

Index

Roasted Tomato Soup 102
Scallop Chowder 79
Seafood Chowder 147
Thai Peanut Soup 75

Steak and Kidney Pie 125
Steamed Rye Brown Bread 72
Stewed Oysters on the Half Shell 50
Stewed Steak with Vegetables 58
Strawberries in Puff Pastry with Chantilly Cream and
    Chocolate Sauce 85

strawberry
One-Two-Three-Four Cake 18
Strawberries in Puff Pastry with Chantilly Cream and
    Chocolate Sauce 85
Strawberry Yogurt Custard with Pepper and Apple Jelly
    Glaze 82
Sugar Cookies with Fruited Buttercream Filling 139

sweet potato
Sweet Potato Tart with Maple-Glazed Pecan and Bacon 163
Warm Roasted Sweet Potato and Chorizo Salad 144

T
Thai Peanut Soup 75
Three-Curry Lobster 67
Three-in-One Rolls 122
Try these Smoked Beef Brisket Sandwiches 155

V
vegetable dishes
Creole Baby Potatoes 93
Dragon's Breath Blue Cheese Corn Bake 171
Roasted Cauliflower with Smoked Gouda Sauce 53
Savory Dill and Garlic Potatoes 54

W
Warm Roasted Sweet Potato and Chorizo Salad 144
Whole Wheat Cranberry Bread 129

wine (red)
Deconstructed Shepherd's Pie 61
Plums Preserved in Mulled Wine 45
Stewed Steak with Vegetables 58
Lunenburg Fruitcake 76
Luskinign 168

Winter Salad 143